"It's easy, Edna, it's downhill all the way."

by Edna Strand Dercum

SIRPOS Press

Contents

1

The Summer of '42

> You wind your way down that trucker's nightmare
> which is Loveland Pass, headed west. Just as the night-
> mare aspect stops and you are becoming reasonably con-
> fident that the highway is not, after all, going to do you
> in, you see a small sign on the left:
> SKI TIP RANCH—1 MILE
> There's a dirt road leading back toward the mountains.
> Take it. Go find out what the world of skiing was like
> before it became programmed entertainment.
> John Jerome in *SKIING Magazine,* 1969

Twenty-seven years earlier my husband and I and our three-months-old baby, Rolf, were winding our way down that "trucker's nightmare." It was the middle of June 1942 and it had snowed eight inches the night before. As I looked over the edge of the winding road to the valley 3,000 feet below, I said to myself, no one will ever catch me driving this pass!

Heading west, we had left the rolling green hills of Pennsylvania where Max had been a Professor of Forestry at Penn State. Our future home was to be Colorado, where, sometime, somehow, and someway we would build a ski lodge, go skiing every day, and live an uninvolved quiet life in the mountains. Little did we dream what lay ahead for us.

Our "covered wagon" was our 1940 Ford convertible. Passing through Oberlin, Ohio, I wondered what Colorado would be like. We

1

had spent most of our lives in suburbia, Max in Cleveland and I in Minneapolis. As we left the East with stately elms, and everything in summer bloom, I felt sure that Dillon, Colorado (elevation 9,500 feet) would be just as lovely at this time of year.

After the rolling hills of Ohio, Illinois, and Missouri we were soon speeding along the main gravel highway of Kansas reaching straight to the horizon and infinity. On the car radio the Denver station was announcing, "From the foot of the towering Rockies..." I pictured a backdrop of steeply rising jagged peaks with glaciers and waterfalls plunging to the edge of Denver.

Clouds were building up around us. As we passed through Oberlin, Kansas, I remarked to Max that I'd never seen such beautiful thunderheads. The wind was terrific. I expected the canvas roof of our little car would rip off at any moment, but we kept sailing on. About two hours later the western music was interrupted by a news flash. "A tornado has just passed through Oberlin, Kansas, leaving much destruction." I drew a deep breath and looked back at the enormous thunderheads we were leaving behind us.

Luckily, we reached Denver at night, and continued up to Idaho Springs, so I missed the expected glaciers and waterfalls. We found a room in a boarding house and decided to go on to Dillon the next morning. Max's new job with the U.S. Forest Service did not start until Monday, and this was Saturday. We would have enough time for him to show me our "ranch" which he had bought the summer before. We had been afraid that America's imminent involvement in the war in Europe would prevent our getting west very soon again to look for land.

Max's job would place him on top of Mt. Evans and the Forest Service took a dim view of a new baby living at an elevation over 14,000 feet. Therefore, I was to stay in Idaho Springs until our furniture arrived. We planned that I would then look around for a house to rent near Dillon, and perhaps begin to fix up our ranch house.

As we neared Dillon Max told me there were four bars and two liquor stores on the one-and-a-half blocks of Dillon's main street, but the bars served breakfast.

A swirling eddy of dust stirred by a cold breeze preceded us as we entered the unpaved main street. Buildings with rough wooden board-walks in front of them lined each side of the street. Each building had a false front, something I had not seen before except in western movies. I looked up and down the street. There were the Blue River Inn, the Dillon Inn, the post office, the grocery store, the Mint Saloon, a tiny drug store, two liquor stores, and a filling station.

Across the street was a one-room-wide house with a false front so high and wide that it overpowered the little, faded-yellow house which appeared to be tipping forward into the street. Tacked onto the back of this house was one little caboose-like room after another, like a train pull-ing the whole building the other direction into the sagebrush field behind the house. On the false front was printed in big letters, "CAFE." But it was empty and closed.

Next to the yellow house, and separated by dirt, sand, and rocks was a series of small, unpeeled-log cabins. There was no grass anywhere. A sign in front of the cabins read, "HEART OF THE ROCKIES CABIN CAMP." A big white heart was painted in the middle of the sign.

For Sunday breakfast we decided to try the nearest bar, the Dillon Inn. It was dim and cool inside with a juke box playing cowboy songs. The jangling of several slot machines lined up near the front of the long room competed with the juke box. The men ignored us as we climbed up on the stools before the bar. We would have preferred one of the booths in the back but they were both occupied. No one else was eating breakfast. There was one menu for six bits (75¢)—steak, eggs, and hash browns. I had never heard of hash browns but felt too timid to inquire.

While waiting to be served we observed the other patrons. They were all having drinks. The bartender set the bottle in front of the customer who poured his own. I heard the bartender say to one fellow down the bar who looked like a miner, "You plannin' on takin' a bath?" I was puzzled, but later learned that when a customer poured himself too generous a drink, that was the usual sarcastic remark.

On all sides of the barroom walls I saw excellent western paintings. I asked the bartender who had done them. "Some guy by name of

Delano," he told me. "Don't know why there are so many exceptin' maybe he bought his grub and booze with 'em." Years later, after Gerard Delano became famous, we saw one of his smaller paintings priced at $15,000.

Steak, eggs, and fried potatoes were served on a thick white-crackled plate with a big mug of coffee. We had almost finished when the slot machine and juke box din was joined by loud swearing toward the back near the booths. Soon we heard blows and more cussing. We started to look around, but the bartender leaned over to us and said, "Don't look around. Just sit tight." Sitting tight on a high wobbly stool isn't easy while holding a squirming baby on your lap and eating with a great curiosity about the barroom drama behind you.

Soon, the battle behind us came closer. "Bam! Bam!" Then we felt a rush of cool air. They'd gone right out the front door and onto the street. We jumped down and looked out. There they were, two big guys slugging it out in the middle of the dirt road that was U.S. Highway 6. In seconds it was a "crowd-gatherer."

Two official looking men came through the crowd, pushing people back and holding up their hands to stop the trucks and cars before they crashed into the crowd. The bartender, leaning over our shoulders, explained. "One's the sheriff and t'other's the marshall." Now, I thought, they'll put a stop to this fight in a hurry. No such thing. They pushed the crowd back enough to give the sluggers room. "It's a fair fight, folks. It's a fair fight, so let 'em finish it. Just stand back, folks." The truck drivers were craning their necks out of their cabs and people in cars behind them were honking their horns. I thought, this is Dillon?

How it ended, I don't know. With Rolf on my hip, I returned to my breakfast at the bar. Soon we took off in our Ford. Our 80-acre ranch that Max had bought the summer before was our destination. I was more than eager to see it. We retraced our route back to the western foot of Loveland Pass to the sign, "Montezuma Road and Montezuma Town—6 Miles." Max explained, "Montezuma is almost at timberline. It's an old mining town in a beautiful valley with a few mining families still living there. There's a boarding house, but I don't know if it's open yet. Idaho

4

Dimp and Lula drive me up to see Montezuma.

My $8.00 a month home across from the Mint.

Mainstreet outhouse, Dillon—turn of the century.

5

Springs is not so high and a lot nearer Mt. Evans, so maybe it will be better if you and Rolf stay there."

We turned off Montezuma road onto a narrow dirt road leading to Dimp Myers' place. Max had told me that the Myers would be our only neighbors for five miles in any direction. At the end of this road I could see a two-story log cabin with a small fence surrounding a neat yard. There was a big barn of unpainted, but beautifully weathered wood. Three goats were warming themselves in the morning sun. We circled around behind the house.

Dimp Myers, our tall and rather gaunt neighbor was standing on the back porch. At first I thought he had a white beard. But then I saw he was in the process of shaving. An enamel basin filled with water stood on a rough wood table. Swinging in the breeze above it was a small mirror.

Alongside the house and under a brightly-painted red shed ran a two-foot wide irrigation ditch lined with green grass and wild flowers. It was filled to the brim with sparkling fast-rushing water. In the shed the Myers kept their cheeses and goats milk.

"Howdy, folks," Dimp greeted us. "So, this is the Missus?" As I shook hands with my new neighbor-to-be, the kitchen screen door banged open and there was Lula.

Lula was long and lanky, as tall as her husband. Her abrupt movements and short brown hair belied the fact that she was in her sixties. In one arm she took Rolf and with the other gave me a big hug. "Come on in and stay for lunch. Then we'll all go to a musical in Frisco." My bewilderment showed immediately. I'd heard that people in the West thought nothing of traveling miles for their entertainment such as driving two or three hundred miles to get to an auction sale or square dance, but Frisco? Max laughed, "Frisco is just a couple of miles beyond Dillon, not San Francisco, Edna."

Anyway, we thanked them, but explained that we were eager to see our ranch as I had not yet seen the place where we would likely live for the rest of our lives. Promising to come back soon, we headed up the road toward Montezuma.

I was very excited. This would be my first sight of our new home. As

6

we turned in at the drive I saw a small grove of tall straight pines in front of a two-story log house. Behind the house were several small log outbuildings, but these were almost dwarfed by a towering spruce tree and thick groves of aspens just beginning to show their new mint-green leaves.

The main log house, I noticed, was of hand-hewn squared timbers that were beautifully dovetailed. The rock foundation was neatly built of flat gray-brown shale. The once-white front door with two curved window panels was nailed tightly shut with boards over the glass. The windows also were all boarded up, even the small loft ones on the second story. Attached to the back of the house, with a clinging look, was a sort of lean-to, and connected to this was a long log building with the bark curling and peeling off the logs.

As I gingerly opened the door of the lean-to room, mice fanned out in all directions, some of them skidding on the grimy linoleum which had been laid down over a dirt floor. I was so repulsed by the idea of living with a hoard of mice, I slammed the door shut, deciding not to explore more just then. I was very much afraid that Max might find out my thoughts. This was to be our *home.* We had burned all our eastern bridges behind us, investing all our money in this ranch.

The other small log buildings were a goat shed, a chicken coop, a sort of a barn shed open on one end for putting up hay, a lean-to for horses, and two log buildings for ranch equipment and vehicles. Also, there was a big roof held up by four sturdy tall posts for protecting hay from rain and snow. A sloping hill led us down to the meadow.

Max explained that in the silver-mining years the ranch had been a stopover for the miners, not only to rest themselves, but also their horses and burros. The animals were fed hay that was cut in these meadows each fall.

Walking around overturned rusting cars, a baby buggy, remains of an old rotting hay wagon, and a sofa with the springs sticking out, I felt depressed. There wasn't a single blade of grass!

"What do we do for water?" I asked apprehensively. Max took me around the back, east of the ranch house, and there was a well with a little peaked roof. I took hold of the rope pully to see how much water I could pull up. The wheel squeaked from lack of use, but up came a bucket splashing water over its rim with a dead chipmunk floating on top! I let go of the rope. The bucket splashed back down out of sight. No way would I use that well!

"Where's the privy?" I wanted to know. Max pointed toward a cluster of small spruce and aspens. Nestled among them was a good-sized board and batten building, but it was quite a distance away. I could not see myself wading through deep snow in winter, let alone wandering out there at night in summer with skunks, bears, and who-knows-what-else prowling around. "We could put up a light, couldn't we? So it wouldn't be so scary to go out at night?" Max laughed, "Honey, the nearest electricity is seven miles away, at Dillon."

"Let's go inside," said Max, leading the way to the back door of the main cabin. Another scramble of mice occurred as he opened the door of the lean-to kitchen.

We went up two steps and entered a darkened narrow hall with a steep staircase on one side that led to two loft rooms. At the end of the hall was the front door and on either side were doors leading to two good-sized rooms. Layers of wall paper hung from the log walls, but the original wood floors were in excellent condition.

"This could be fixed up—at least to live in for awhile," I said as hopefully as possible, wondering if we could afford a new well and pump.

"Well, now you know what it looks like, we'd better head back to Idaho Springs," said Max. It really was a beautiful location, and I knew the ever-optimistic Max was never as discouraged as I.

We had been walking around for quite a while and not a car had gone by. "There's not much traffic on this road, is there?" I asked Max. He explained why. Dimp had told him that this place had been a stage-coach stop for travelers coming over Argentine Pass from Georgetown. Later I was to see Argentine Pass and was grateful Loveland Pass had been built in 1937. In the early days before the turn of the century silver was the big thing. Most often the "stage" was just a two-seated horse-drawn wagon. We decided that the long log room attached to the south end of the ranch house had been the blacksmith shop for the stagecoach days. The stone grinding wheel, bellows, and bench with tools and anvils were still in place.

The miners, Dimp had said, would bring their ore-laden burros from the mining camps of Montezuma, Decatur, Saints John, and Chihuahua down here to our ranch. Our place was then known as the "Elwood Placer," and later as "The Black Ranch." Here, they would usually transfer their ore onto the dray wagons which would take the ore to the town of Keystone where the narrow-guage railroad spur came up from Dillon. At Dillon the ore cars would be added to trains headed for the smelters in Leadville. These smelters were built by the Guggenheim brothers who founded their vast fortune in Leadville.

After the graveled U.S. Highway 6 was built over Loveland Pass, the old wagon road which went through Keystone was almost abandoned. Keystone was not a mining town. It formerly had a sawmill, several well-built log cabins, and one good-sized white board-and-batten house. I told Max the big house looked like the neat farm houses I'd seen in Sweden. He told me that Keystone was a logging settlement and the settlers had come from Sweden. They logged the trees cut on Keystone mountain, then "hacked" them into railroad ties or milled them into mine timbers. Lumber was hauled up the old Montezuma wagon road to our place where it was loaded on burros for the mines.

The late afternoon sun cast long shadows as we headed back over Loveland Pass and returned to Idaho Springs where Max had to report in for his Forest Service job.

The next morning as Max walked off with duffel and sleeping bag to the Forest Service office on Miner's Street, I waved until he turned the corner, not knowing when I would see him next. Mt. Evans where he would live until the snows drove him down, is not visible from Idaho Springs as the mountains around the town hide the 14,000-foot peak from view.

Turning back, I went into the big front room Mrs. Marshall had given us in her boarding house. Mrs. Marshall was in her eighties, a short heavyset woman with a deep and often booming husky voice. She saw me as I came in and followed me into the room where Rolf still slept in his small portable bed.

"I know it's hard for you and you're worried, but tell you what," she continued, "I can let you have this room for $3.50 a week. Can't go any lower." I was astounded, knowing it was a $25.00 a week room. All the while she was talking, she had been surreptitiously picking up the diapers and before I could protest she was off to wash them for me.

One afternoon, while sitting on the veranda which faced Main Street, I saw Mrs. Marshall walking up the street with her slow side-to-side gait. "Where have you been?" I asked.

"Had to go to Denver to see the Guvner."

"Weren't you rather in awe of seeing the Governor? Did you really get to see him?" I asked.

"Course I did," she answered as she lowered herself into a squeaking rocker. "Didn't like some of the things going on in the government and thought I'd tell him. And as for being afraid, or in awe, as you puts it, land sakes, I used to give him jam and bread. He grew up just across the street. Good kid, but needed a spanking now and then. I helped out on that too, sometimes." I'd never met anyone who dared scold a governor!

Several days later the notice came that our furniture had arrived not at Idaho Springs, but at a town named Kremmling. Where on earth is Kremmling? I wondered. I asked Mrs. Marshall and she told me it was on U.S. 40 over Berthoud Pass, through Winter Park, and Hot Sulphur Springs. It was about a hundred miles away, but only 40 miles north of Dillon.

"I've never driven over a mountain pass," I said.

"This one's paved and not as high as Loveland, a bit under timberline," she assured me. The moving company notice had taken its own good time in getting to me. A small notation on the bottom stated, "Must be picked up by July 1, no later." And this was June 30th!

"I'd better go first thing in the morning," I told Mrs. Marshall.

Bright and early I was ready to leave with Rolf ensconced in the back seat happily exploring his toes. As I watched him play, I reflected that I'd better be just as nonchalant. Berthoud Pass, I discovered to my delight, was no problem. I even found I could enjoy the magnificent scenery. There were big snowfields with huge overhanging cornices. What fun to ski down that, I thought, not knowing a thing about avalanches. Winding down, down into the valley I came to Winter Park, a famous ski area I'd read about in the American Ski Annual. I parked the car at the side of the road and looked up at the T-bar lift and the ski trails. They looked steep and long to me. I wondered if I'd ever get to ski there. But I must hurry on and figure out what to do with our furniture. From Winter Park the mountains receded on both sides and the valley became wider and lonelier.

Arriving at Kremmling, I found the Railway Express Station in the old railroad building on the tracks beside the Colorado River. This day was my first view of that famous river, starting as a small creek in the mountains I'd just come over. Eventually it goes all the way through the Grand Canyon and on to California and Mexico. Here, it flowed along slowly and gently through green mountain meadows.

To find an unfriendly person was not what I expected. In the express window a sour-faced fellow looked at my notice card and said, "You've got till tomorrow to get your furniture out. And, here's your bill." The bill was huge, $142! I would have only $10 left.

"How will I get this hauled to Dillon?" I asked. "Dunno, lady. That's your problem." He pulled the slatted wooden window down in my face. I walked into the storage place where the furniture was stacked. Everything was crated, even my dust mop. No wonder it had cost so much! But, where were Max's and my skis? I knocked at the window that had just been slammed down in my face.

"My skis?" I shouted at him. "Where are they?"

"Probably got put off in Chicago." Grudgingly he said he would send a tracer.

My heart was already in my shoes. Only $10.00 left and Max up at 14,000 feet with no phone. I would have no more money until he got his check of $90.00 at the end of the month from the Forest Service. Actually there would be only $80.00 after they took out his rent. And now our skis were lost.

I drove to a dusty side street to park and nurse my baby. I cried pretty hard, and wondered, What do I do now? Well, I thought, it's not going to help sitting here. I drove to the town square and looked around. Two women were gossiping outside a newly-painted building with big red letters on the false front, "Del Rio Cafe." The cafe wasn't open so I approached the women.

"Does anyone haul freight to Dillon?"

"Well," one of the women said while looking me up and down, "that fellow over there talking to the blacksmith might haul to Dillon, seeing as how he lives there."

The other woman smiled at me and asked, "You a wife of one of them ski troopers from Camp Hale?"

"Oh, no," I answered. "My husband is working for the Forest Service."

"That there is Roy Kohl talking to the blacksmith whose name is Dan Hoare." With this information I approached the two men. How was I going to tell them I had only a $10 traveler's check besides some change and a few bills?

I blurted it out, my whole story. They could hear Rolf starting to cry in the car. Mr. Kohl broke into a big grin and said, "I usually haul coal to Dillon, but I'll meet you at eight in the morning on the main street of Dillon and you can tell me where you want the furniture. And it'll only cost you ten dollars." I could have hugged him, in fact hugged all of them, including the woman who had lifted Rolf out of the back seat and was bouncing him up and down much to his glee.

Arriving in Idaho Springs late that afternoon I was elated until suddenly I realized, I don't have a house. But, I'll get up early and contact the Dillon Forest Ranger. He'd been so kind to Max the summer before. Maybe I'd better leave Rolf with Mrs. Marshall and get over to Dillon tonite to see if I can find a house.

"Sure I'll take care of Rolfy," Mrs. Marshall assured me, making it possible for me to leave right away for Dillon. It was getting dusk when I reached Dillon's main street. I parked the car in front of the Heart of the Rockies Cabin Camp. Whenever someone went in or out of the bars I could hear honky-tonk music blending with the ring of slot machines.

An old cowboy was standing across the street in front of a building announcing itself as the "MINT SALOON." I walked over and asked him if he knew where I might be able to rent a small house. "The guy who owns most of the town is in there, Old Man Riley," he said while pointing with his thumb over his shoulder to the door of the Mint. I entered slowly, and for the first time I felt a bit afraid. In Pennsylvania women didn't go into bars. I doubted that they even had any bars like this. Maybe they didn't have any bars at all.

Three men were sitting at a small round table playing poker. They were wearing cowboy hats shoved back on their heads. I remember thinking, how strange, they all have such white foreheads. I later noticed that cowboys' faces are tan only up to their hat brims, leaving a definite boundary line when, if ever, they took off their hats.

I was surprised I could speak at all when I asked, "Mr. Riley?"

"Yup, wadda ya want?" The older of the three men looked at me. Gratefully, I realized his manner was not unkind.

"I need to rent a house, not a big one," I told him.

"You can have the one across the street." He pointed to the small, false-fronted house. "It'll cost you $8.00 a month." I told him I had a little baby and all about Max working for the Forest Service on top of Mt. Evans. The Forest Service had said it was too dangerous to bring a small baby to live at that altitude. I explained he'd have to wait a bit for the $8.00 as I had spent my last traveler's check getting my furniture hauled up from Kremmling.

I waited while all three men looked at me without saying anything. Then all of a sudden Mr. Riley grinned and said, "That's O.K. by me. It's almost July so what about paying the $8.00 on August first?" He gave me the key and I happily went across the street to my new abode.

A five-foot-wide boardwalk ran the length of the housefront. I opened the door right into the front room, and reached automatically for

Spring   Rolf Dercum

The sudden warming
   of the ground after winter
Spring is a teasing hint of green
   in our high mountain valley
From the wet and muddy earth
   tiny green shoots push up

Sap rises into the new growth
Willows show a wide span of color
   yellow green, purple red
A bursting restlessness
   in the constantly changing
   light of spring

the switch. Thank God, it has electricity. A cord with a single light bulb hung from the ceiling. A big window faced right on the street. When I opened the door, I found that two steps beyond the boardwalk would put me right on the main street, U.S. Highway 6.

The front room was long and narrow. Beyond it was the kitchen, and then a bedrom big enough for twin beds, a dresser, and Rolf's little bed. From the kitchen there was a door opening to a long, dark shed used for wood and coal storage. Beyond the coal shed was the privy, a two-holer. Later, I was to find out that this was a communal convenience I would share with the "guests" of the Heart of the Rockies cabin camp next door. Fortunately it had a good strong inside bolt.

After returning to Idaho Springs, I fell into bed exhausted, but before I fell asleep I thought, just a few days ago I told myself that no one would ever catch me driving these passes. And here I've driven over two of them, and twice in one day.

I'd set my alarm for five a.m. so that we would be off in plenty of time to arrive at the main street of Dillon to guide the truck to the house. I reached Dillon at seven a.m. thinking I would have to wait. But no, to the side of the house was piled the crating from the furniture. Inside were Mr. Kohl and Jake Jauch, the forest ranger, hooking up my refrigerator. Everything was in place, even the beds and Rolf's crib set up in the bedroom. "I'll bring your skis when they get to Kremmling," Mr. Kohl assured me.

"How did you ever get in?" I asked.

"Oh, Mr. Riley was here and opened up and he'd told most folk in town you'd need help." From the grocery store directly across the street came a plump jolly-looking woman. "This here is Irma Feaster, Mrs. Dercum," Mr. Kohl introduced us. "She runs the grocery store." Irma took Rolf from my arms, settled herself in a comfortable chair, and told me, "You've no need to worry about paying for groceries for a month."

I laughed happily, "Thanks, Irma. I don't think I'll be lonely here. That's what I was afraid of the most."

That night I wrote to Max to tell him all that had happened in just two days. "I'll drive out to the ranch," I wrote, "and see what I can do to

14

clean up around there. Maybe I can get the irrigation ditch going.''

And to my mother in Minnesota, ''I really wish you were here. I know you would like this crazy old town with such friendly people. It's a far cry from Minnesota, not to mention Penn State. You would believe you are back in Norway in the mountains you miss so much.''

The next morning at the post office I was delighted to find a letter from Max forwarded from the Idaho Springs Forest Service office. It had taken him almost all day to get up to Mt. Evans following the big rotary snowplow. Max wrote about getting settled for the summer, contacting visitors, fire detection, hauling lumber, and living with some interesting research scientists. Max's last paragraph made me wish Rolf and I could join him:

> *I have seen bighorn sheep several times (a ram with five ewes) less than 100 feet away, and for 15 minutes at a time. Today from the peak I heard several bull elk whistling. Have seen marmots and coneys in the rocks. They are fun to watch. At night Denver lies below us like a giant glittering tiara. Miss you. Love, Max.*

Early one morning, just about a week after I'd moved to Dillon, I was awakened by the sound of gun shots. They sounded quite close so I rushed to the front window. There across the street on the board walk in front of the Mint Saloon sat two cowboys aiming their rifles right at my house. I jumped back, terrified, and tore into the bedroom. I'd better get dressed in case I should need help and have to run out the back way through the sage brush.

But the shots had stopped. Peeking out the window again, I saw the door of the Mint swing shut behind the two men. The grocery door was open, so I rushed across the street and breathlessly burst in on Irma.

''Irma,'' I panted, ''did you hear those shots? Those cowboys were shooting at my house!''

To my amazement Irma started laughing. ''Honey,'' she was almost choking with laughter, ''they weren't shooting at your house. Most every

15

Sunday morning they try to ring the church bell. See? Right over the top of your house?'' I looked and sure enough there was the church bell tower in plain view beyond my house across the sagebrush field.

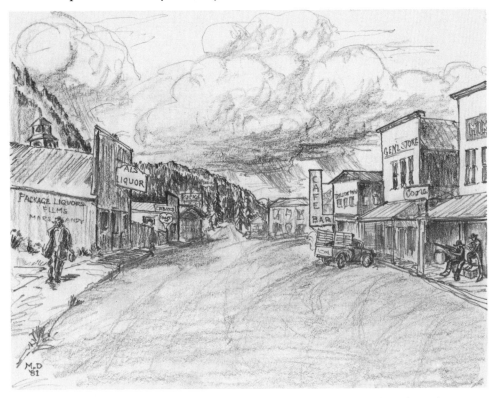

I had also noticed the two-room schoolhouse near the church. Now, I walked around behind the house and looked at it. Oh no, I thought. My children will grow up and go to that? Two rooms for eight grades! For the first time, I felt apprehensive about the future. Without sensing the first bit of snobbery in myself, I thought, there must be a bigger and surely much better school somewhere near here.

A couple of days later when I was fixing lunch, the door opened and there stood Bestemor, my little Norwegian mother! ''But how did you get

16

here?'' I asked with great relief, bursting into tears. I suddenly realized I wouldn't be alone any more.

Bestemor said, ''Max wrote to me and invited me to come. He told me, 'When you get off the bus just ask anyone in Dillon and they'll tell you where Edna and Rolf are.' And what's all that lumber at the side of the house, Edna? It looks bad thrown out like that. And when do I see Rolf?''

Early the next morning I heard strange sounds outside the bedroom window. I'd forgotten my mother's habit of getting up at 5 a.m. I looked out the window and there was Bestemor in a big floppy sun hat sitting on a log stump she'd found in the coal shed. She had located the tire jack in the Ford, and was vigorously pulling the nails out of the crating and stacking the lumber neatly. A couple of days later when I found it all gone she informed me that she had sold it to Mr. Riley, only she called him ''Old Man Raelly'' in her Norwegian accent. Then she handed me a receipt for two month's rent. ''It was a gud trade,'' she said with satisfaction.

With the 87th Infantry stationed at Camp Hale just beyond Leadville, the bars in Dillon were doing a bang-up business. The ski troopers crowded in every evening, and the honky-tonk pianos vied with the ring of the slot machines. I was soon to learn the meaning of ''camp-followers,'' and ''red-light district,'' and ''rolling the soldiers.''

Getting off the bus one afternoon were two good-looking girls, dressed quite elaborately for Dillon, I thought. They were carrying heavy suitcases as they picked their way in their high-heeled shoes across the dusty main street and into the Heart of the Rockies next door. One, with heavy brown curls cascading to her shoulders, was wearing a fur jacket though the temperature was 80°. I assumed they must be on a misguided travel agency holiday.

Irma's grocery store was the best place to find out what was going on in town. The outside national and world news stayed outside. I often wondered if we were still at war. No one talked of anything except the Saturday night dance, or why some drunk decided to try to kill himself by driving 90 miles an hour up and down main street until he ran out of gas.

Then, rather than fill up the car, he'd fill himself up again at one of the bars. And there, everyone knew, the sheriff would grab him.

Soon I heard, by taking my time in the grocery store, that the two new girls in town were waitressing at the Blue River Saloon. None of this much interested me except, since my bedroom window faced on the back of the "H of R" cabins, I was kept awake or awakened late at night by loud laughter and a wind-up phonograph playing cowboy laments. One refrain I remember best as it was played over and over, "Why don't cha haul off and love me like ya ust ta do," with the emphasis on "haul off." Realizing by then what "camp-followers" meant, I just wished they had found lodgings somewhere else and far away.

For several weeks and during the day, I had noticed a little girl about ten years old, standing in front of the grocery store. She had long blond hair, and would have been quite pretty if she hadn't been so terribly thin. I asked Irma who the child was. She told me she was the daughter of a woman who lived about a half mile out of town in an old cabin. The mother was crippled from polio and sent the child in for groceries. The father, Irma had heard, worked in South Dakota during the threshing season and got back before winter set in. "You'll notice," said Irma, "how she follows those two gals around,—the ones staying over at the cabins next to your place."

I didn't think much more about any of this since I'd gotten a bike and could take off to the ranch, or visit my new friends at the Forest Service ranger station. Some days I would bicycle for miles admiring the fields of wild flowers in the valley. Having Bestemor there with Rolf gave me so much more freedom.

One morning I was giving Rolf his bath in front of the kitchen window which faced the cabins and I saw a green sedan pull up in front of them. There were two men in the front seat. Glancing at the license plate, I noticed it was from Illinois. Soon, one of the young girl waitresses came running out and got in the back seat, slamming the door. I thought they would take off but they sat there for quite awhile with the motor idling. Then the second girl came out holding the hand of the little blond child I'd seen hanging around town. The little girl was dressed in a bright red

18

satin dress far too big for her but pulled up by some kind of belt. She kept tripping over the too-long dress and stumbled along in the much too big high heeled slippers she was wearing. She would have fallen if the girl holding her hand hadn't supported her. Since she was laughing delightedly, I thought, poor kid. They are letting her play dress-up and probably taking her along on a picnic.

Bestemor and Rolf and I drove that afternoon to Idaho Springs to visit Mrs. Marshall and we stayed overnight. I hadn't returned home for more than ten minutes when the lady caretaker from the cabins next door came shuffling through the dust in her felt slippers. Irma had just dropped by to check that all was okay with us. I put on the coffee pot wondering why all of a sudden the visitors—and in the morning, too. Irma, though, often came over to sit near the window in the warm east sun, bouncing Rolf on her knee while keeping an eye open for any customers coming into the store.

"Ain't it a terrible thing, that kidnapping?" the woman from the cabin camp exclaimed.

"What kidnapping?" I asked.

"Just two days ago," she went on, "those gals who rented one of my cabins took off and it's believed they took that poor woman's child with 'em."

"What?" I shouted. "Do you mean when they put her in that car they were kidnapping her? I thought they were probably just going on a picnic."

"You mean you saw them take her away and you saw the car?" asked Irma. "The sheriff's been asking if anyone saw anything. We've got to let him know, Edna."

"Would one of you call him?" I asked. "I don't even know who the sheriff is." I felt sad and frightened and wondered where the poor little girl was now.

It was about supper time when the sheriff knocked. With him was a tall man I had not seen around Dillon.

"Mrs. Dercum," the sheriff said, "this here's Mr. Grant, the District Attorney from Leadville, and we understand you saw the kidnapping?"

19

"And just why didn't you report it?" Mr. Grant asked in a very quiet voice, a voice that sounded almost threatening.

"For one thing, Mr. Grant, I didn't realize it was a kidnapping. Also, the little girl had been hanging around and following those women for about a month. I thought they were just humoring her, dressing her up in their clothes and letting her come along on a picnic. It was in the morning before lunch and in broad daylight too," I exclaimed.

"Well," said the sheriff, "you'll be glad to know the gals have been caught in Utah and the child has been returned to her mother. They're in jail in Leadville. Got no woman's jail in this county."

"But," Mr. Grant broke in, "we'll be needing you for a witness. Seems as if they were with a white slave ring." He continued, "It seems funny to me that you waited so long telling anyone what you saw. And, by the way, where's your husband? Are you sure now, that you didn't know these gals before you came here?"

I was speechless. But not my mom. She'd been listening and sitting quietly at the far end of the living room. But, at the last question she stood up, straight and erect, all four-feet-ten-inches of her, and glared at the men. "You yust get out of hare," she stated in her strong Norwegian accent.

They looked astounded but the sheriff grinned, got up and walked out leaving the flustered district attorney to follow.

But I was worried. I thought, what if it's a gang? That was an Illinois license plate and those women were from California. I've read about "silencing" witnesses. My mother must have noted my worry because she said, "I must tell you what my Finnish grandmother once told me. It is from the old Finnish *Kalevala* and I never forgot it." She quoted, " 'The witless one lies awake all night and worries and in the morning his woe is just as it was.' "

So, I went to bed and slept soundly. In the morning the sheriff knocked at my door. "You'll be glad to know, Mrs. Dercum, that those two gals confessed, so you won't be needed as a witness. And I apologize to both of you for worrying you." I laughed with relief and told him, "I guess my mom took care of the worrying part, so it wasn't all that bad."

20

Max wrote me enthusiastically about his life on Mt. Evans:

Since being up here it seems every day has been different and certainly not monotonous. I stay in the University of Denver Cosmic Ray Lab, above the concession house, with two fellows from the University of Chicago who are doing research on cosmic rays. One is Professor Ralph Lapp, who is quite well-known in the physics field. The other day I met a most interesting fellow, Enrico Fermi, who has been going down to the foot of the cliff and diving into the ice cold waters of the lake. He has scuba diving equipment and has been measuring cosmic rays in the water. Also, he told us, he has gone deep into some of the mines doing the same thing. One of the fellows here is from Brazil, and there are a Dr. Nielson and his wife from University of California, who are both physicists.

The concession is open and there are always many cars at a time up here. Sundays are extremely busy and I make public contacts all day explaining the activities of the Forest Service. I have also been hauling lumber and other materials to the lower point, east of where we climbed and have started construction of a little shelter for the fire finder, radio and myself. Howard Lee, the Forest Service ranger, says 70 percent of my work will be public contacts, the rest fire detection. I'm to come down to the concession and the trailer whenever lightning storms threaten. Up here on Mt. Evans in the last several days it has been beautifully warm, freezing cold, foggy with no visibility, clear as a bell with visibility of 150 miles, snowing for several hours, rain, wind you'd think could blow the buildings right off the mountain, and one night with lightning striking all around us.

I was glad Max had such a fantastic setting and interesting people around as I knew he was missing seeing Rolf grow this summer.

Early mornings in Dillon it was often 15 to 30 degrees with frost on the roofs. The air practically crackled it was so crisp and clear. The sky was an unbelievable deep blue. With a slight breeze the laundry would dry in minutes.

Max wrote to me that he might go "to the west coast and work in the logging there which has A-1 priority for the Nation's war needs. Much timber is needed for docks, shipbuilding, and piling. Of course that is unless I am drafted."

In August I wrote Max:

> *I have been trying to buy a 375-acre ranch which almost adjoins ours. It is at the foot of Loveland Pass and is called the Frye Ranch. Mr. Frye, who lives in Golden, wants $5,000 for it. His sister said they would take $4,500. Remember that your grandmother said she would loan us that amount? Do you think we should accept her offer? With the war on I don't know where we will be and how long the war will last. We might not get back here for ten years or more. I sometimes despair we'll ever get back. I've learned to love it here so much, the valley, the mountain, and the people.*

When large produce and other trucks came through town, they had to make a sharp right-angle turn at the Dillon Inn. One early morning in September, I was lying in bed half awake, when I heard the sound of a big truck heading toward town from the south. I could tell by its approach that it was coming much too fast to make the turn at the Inn.

Jumping out of bed, I ran to the front window just as it roared past. The driver threw on the brakes but it didn't do much good as it skidded sideways and then turned over at the junction, just missing the Conoco gas station and Erick Erickson's log house. The truck was loaded with peaches. As the trailer part of the truck slowly tipped sideways, the peaches poured out. I grabbed my bathrobe, slippers, and a washtub, and tore out of the door. From the doors up and down main street and the side streets came women who flew along with colorful or drab bathrobes

22

pulled over their shoulders, all carrying wash tubs, and converging on the hapless truck.

In no time at all the peaches disappeared, and so did all the women. The truck driver was O.K., but his screaming at all of us women was to no avail.

August went by and September came. Every day I was expecting word from Max about our plans for the coming winter. With great delight one chilly morning in September I saw Max alight from a Forest Service pickup as it pulled up in front of my boardwalk.

He wasn't even in the door before he started telling me, "Too much snow on Mt. Evans, so I've been moved down to Squaw Mountain about 15 miles north. It's only around 12,000 feet high. Since the forestry student who has been manning the lookout there has to return to college, I've been asked to be the lookout until the snows definitely drive us down."

"Us? You mean we can live there too?" I was beside myself with joy. "It works out beautifully here in Dillon," Max continued, "because the forest ranger and his wife want Bestemor to look after their two children at the ranger's house. Shorty, the ranger's wife, has been offered a part-time job. She's a nurse, you know." Bestemor was pleased about the prospect because she really enjoyed the Jauch family.

Piling what we thought we would need into the car after arranging to store our furniture in Dillon, off we went.

2

Three on the Lookout

It was dark when we reached Idaho Springs, but we had to get up to Squaw Mountain since Max was to start his fire lookout duty at seven a.m. the next morning.

The rocky dirt road seemed endless, but we finally came to a dead end and a turnaround. "You had better stay here with Rolf until I get the stove going," Max advised. "Then I'll come back and guide you."

The stars were brilliant in a black sky which was all I could see from the side of the mountain. It seemed as if Max was gone forever. I began wondering what was keeping him when I looked up and saw red sparks in the sky. Realizing this was from the stove I almost panicked. We're going way up there in the dark?

Soon I could see a small light bobbing along as Max returned with a lantern. As I stepped out of the car the wind tore at my coat and almost bowled me over. I picked up Rolf who was sound asleep in his bundle of blankets. We started up a narrow trail which zigzagged through huge rocks. Finally we came up against a stone wall which turned out to be the base of the lookout. Max led the way around one side and then up a steep stairway and onto a balcony. With the wind pushing at us, it was all we could do to open the door and get into the lookout. It was one room, about 18 feet square with huge plate glass windows all around.

I had never seen such a sight. I was thrilled. It seemed all of Denver was glittering right below us to the east. I looked to the north and there, 4000 feet straight down, was the mainstreet of Idaho Springs. It was both exhilarating and frightening.

Max made two more trips down to the car to bring up Rolf's bed and the groceries. In the light of the Coleman lantern I made up the double bed built right into the wall under the south windows. A counter ran around two sides with cupboards below and part of the counter was a desk. This would have to double as our dining area. There was a small wood cooking stove in one corner.

In the middle of the room was the fire finder. I realized then why there were no upper cupboards and no walls anywhere, only glass, so nothing could block out the four-directional view from the fire finder. Later I was to find out just how hot it could get in there when the sun was setting. The wooden shutters which jutted straight out helped during the middle of the day. What I did to create a little shade was undoubtedly *verboten*. I hung a small blanket on a string tied to the stovepipe damper and across to the door. It gave us some shade and made a darn good place to hang laundry.

The next morning I learned more about our mountain aerie. From the fire finder on each side were bent metal legs curving into the floor. Near the finder was a three-legged stool with a glass insulator on each leg. Max explained to me that during the summer, when lightning is striking all around, the forester will sit or stand on this stool so that the balls of fire rolling off the metal legs of the fire finder will not electrocute him. I was glad to hear that the mountain electrical storm season was over. Off toward Kansas and the prairies of eastern Colorado beyond Denver, however, I could see lightning striking. What a strange setting, I thought, and we have a ringside seat.

"Well, little fellow," I said picking up Rolf and tossing him in the air, "you're going to fly the highest diapers in the U.S."

The only phone was a direct line to the Forest Service in Idaho Springs. What was happening in the outside world was unknown to us. We heard no news of the war.

The six weeks up on Squaw Mountain went fast. We had plenty to read, and the ranger from Idaho Springs came up twice bringing us groceries. No visitors, which I didn't mind. Max enjoyed getting acquainted again with our son. We took turns taking the one hike possible to the bench mark, an elevation station on the mountain. This covered a blind area we had to check every day from where we could look down and out for any smokes.

I especially remember a lovely ptarmigan on the trail. He would wait every day for one of us to appear. Then he would start out just enough in front of me to assure that I couldn't touch him. He walked ahead with great dignity, cocking his head, and looking back now and then to make sure I was following. His feathers had already started to turn white for his perfect winter camouflage in the snows to come.

Having been impressed all summer with the wild flowers, I now enjoyed the vivid reds, oranges and ambers of the low shrubs all around us,

26

and the many shades of colors of the lichens on the big gray rocks. Aspens turned to gold on the slopes below us.

Every day it seemed the mornings were crystal clear, but once in awhile in the morning, Denver and the plains to the east would completely disappear in fog. We would look over an ocean of clouds rolling up the gulches of the foothills like huge surf waves. Half an hour later the fog would completely disperse and the sky would be a deep blue without a cloud anywhere.

The balcony completely encircled the building. I would put Rolf out there in his bed for his morning nap. Once as I was tucking him in, a big eagle swooped down under the shutters almost touching my shoulder with his wing. He was magnificent, but frightening.

One morning there was a haze and Max announced, "There's a forest fire off to the northwest. I'd better call it in." Telephoning down to the Idaho Springs ranger station, he was surprised when they told him he must be mistaken. No fire had been reported anywhere. Max insisted that it had to be a big one and he believed it to be over on the Routt National Forest, not far from Steamboat Springs. If it were, he was told, it would have been reported to the main Denver office. All day Max watched the haze and at sunset time he was very upset. "There *is* a forest fire over there, I'm positive," he told me. The next morning the phone woke us early. It was the ranger station. "If Denver calls you don't mention the report you made to us yesterday," they said. "It seems there is a big forest fire just northwest of Steamboat Springs and the regional office will be pretty upset if they hear you called it in yesterday." "Well, glad you finally believe me," Max retorted. And that fire took them two weeks to put out.

We watched the landscape turn into the many autumn colors, like a big Persian carpet spread out below us. One morning we woke to a spitting and hissing noise. Sleet was driving hard against our windows and frost feathers were building up on the wooden shutters. The phone rang. It was the Forest Service office telling us a storm was on the way (as if we couldn't tell) and requesting us to vacate the lookout immediately.

Hoar frost was beginning to crystallize and whiten the balcony. It was a good thing mist and clouds prevented us from seeing the view. That

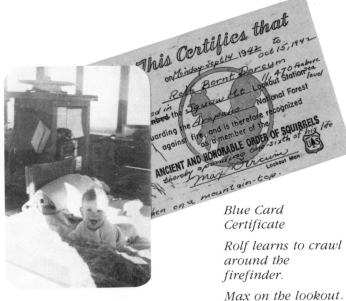

*Blue Card
Certificate*

*Rolf learns to crawl
around the
firefinder.*

Max on the lookout.

*Looking back, I
thought, "Let the
rest of the world go
by."*

28

made it easier to pull down and fasten the already frosted shutters. Hurriedly we bundled all of our belongings, wrapped Rolf well, and started through the storm down over the slippery rock path to the car below. We must have looked like fleeing peasants. I couldn't help laughing to myself at the picture we must have made. I looked back once, hating to leave where we had a most beautiful six weeks. The snow and clouds were already obscuring the lookout as we descended in a swirl of snowflakes.

After checking in at the Forest Service in Idaho Springs we drove on to Dillon and to the Jauch's who had invited us to stay with them when we came down. It was good to see them again and to see Bestemor. The next morning Max and Jake Jauch took their skis and drove up to Loveland Pass for the first skiing of the season.

When I collected our mail in Dillon, among the letters was a small but very welcome check. Just a month before Rolf was born, before we had left Penn State, I had written an article titled, "Forestry Goes Skiing," and had sent it off to a forestry magazine. The reason I had written it was because I had gotten into an argument with one of the forestry professors, who had informed me that skiing had no place in forestry. The magazine had also sent me two copies. I delightedly noticed that the professor was on the board of trustees of that magazine.

An offer for logging in the Northwest materialized so we bought a small trailer and loaded it with what we thought we'd need. Max took me to Denver where Rolf and I boarded the Union Pacific train headed for Portland, Oregon. Then he drove west with the little Ford convertible, hauling the trailer.

The train was crowded and full of soldiers. My departure from Colorado could not have ended with more finality than that day on the train leaving Denver in a glowing sunset. Looking out of the window to the west as the sun was setting, I didn't want to take my eyes off the mountains until I could no longer see them. But the porter came through and pulled all the shades down tightly.

"Couldn't I just keep my shade up awhile?" I asked.

"Sorry, lady, but all the trains gotta be blacked out," he stated. "Don't you know we got a war on?"

The next three years were another sort of blackout time as we'd left our hearts back in the mountains of Colorado. One bright spot was the birth of our daughter, Sunni, born eight months later in Longview, Washington. It was a town on the Columbia River built below the waterline, protected by dikes. Many years later I overheard Sunni say to someone who had just told her she was a bit different, "Oh, that's because I was conceived above timberline and born below sea level."

3

Return to the Summit

The war was over at last. It was October 1945 when we set forth for Colorado.

While in Washington, Max had formed, with two other foresters, a logging company known as Farm Foresters, Inc. Logging was A-1 priority during the war. Often, during those war years, I would pull the children in their little wagon down to the banks of the Columbia River. From there we would watch the huge Russian freighters almost every day loading timbers from the local sawmills. All of this went gratis from the U.S. to the Soviet Union. Sometimes a U.S. ship would be loading pilings used for building bridges. Max liked to think that maybe the pilings he'd logged would be used for our troops, especially the ski troops at the Anzio beachhead in Italy.

Max bought the logging truck and bulldozer, which he called "the cat" (Caterpillar tractor), from the company when it disbanded at the end of the war. He sold his interest in the portable sawmill which had been used to go from farm to farm. This efficient little sawmill was instrumental in setting up some of the first tree farms in the state. Earl Ganong, a skier friend we had met at Longview during this time, ran this small portable mill.

When we weren't tied up with our two little ones Adina Ganong and I would join Max and Earl and drive up to the base of Mt. St. Helens. From there we would climb to the ski club cabin and spend the night. Early the next morning, just as the sun would touch the long white snowy slopes, we would climb and climb. Then we would start the long descent back down to the cabin. Looking today at pictures of Mt. St. Helens, of the devastated area and the collapsed mountain, it is hard to believe we ever skied there.

We had to ship the bulldozer by freight to Kremmling, Colorado. Kremmling, I thought to myself, I sure hope we don't have to confront that depressing freight man who gave me such a hard time on my only other trip to that town.

"Of all the things we have, which are mighty few," Max assured me, "this cat might keep the wolf from our cabin door in Colorado." Little did we dream then that this machine would be the first bulldozer which would help build the early trails and clear the lift line at what was to become the Arapahoe Basin Ski Area the very next summer.

The logging truck was loaded with what furniture we had plus all the canned goods from our war-time Victory Garden. There were boxes of carrots, turnips, blueberries, apples, cherries and even salmon. I took the train with the children while Max drove the logging truck. His dad, wanting to see what Colorado looked like, followed with our little Ford convertible. Trailing behind the Ford was the same two-wheeled trailer with even more stuff. It took them 12 days across the west. They must have made quite a procession.

After my arrival in Boulder, where Bestemor and my sister Martha lived, I awaited Max's phone call from Dillon. It seemed forever. I was so eager to see old Summit County again and all of our good friends up there.

Max and his dad drove down to Boulder, and leaving the children with Bestemor, they drove me back up to Dillon. Dimp and Lula had already decided that we couldn't possibly live at the ranch. There still was no electricity, but that wasn't the real problem. Dimp and Lula didn't have any electricity either. The nearest connection to them was in Dillon six miles away. The ranch house was just too filthy, having been uninhabited during the war. It needed a lot of work to make it liveable.

"It's not fit fer livin' 'ceptin' fer lots of mice, pack rats and squirrels," Lula said. "But, I think the folks up the road about a mile from here want

32

Sunday callers pose with Dimp and Lula.

Rolf's first horse.

After the first October snow; Sunni and Rolf lean their skis against the "Alhambra".

33

to sell their cabin and go to live with their children in Idaho. Let's go talk to 'em."

We drove past our ranch and up the road to a low-roofed cabin nestled against the slope of a steep craggy mountain which we later learned was Porcupine Mountain. The tall dead trees on the ridge made the top of the mountain look like it had sprouted sharp porcupine quills.

The old couple in the cabin welcomed us warmly. There were many unpeeled log sheds around the place plus a big unfinished barn. They showed us the spring nearby where we could get pure clear water. The neat log privy behind the cabin had a brightly-painted green door.

The roof of this little cabin slanted almost to the ground in the rear. The door entered directly into the kitchen and beyond the kitchen were two tiny bedrooms side by side. The log wall was only two feet high at the north end of both bedrooms. The kitchen had three windows, one to the east, one to the south next to the door, and one to the west. The sun could warm this little room which would be our living room and dining room also.

They showed us a trap door in one of the bedrooms with steep steps leading down into a dirt cellar. Here was where they stored all their produce and canned goods and we would too. "You see," Lula explained to me, "if you go to Denver for a few days everything will freeze in the cabin. You gotta store all the stuff you don't want freezin' in the cellar. We call 'em root cellars here and everybody's got one."

Here was a place into which we would move right away. We drove back to Boulder and fetched Bestemor and the children. Bestemor fell in love with the old cabin nestled among the tall Engelmann spruce and lodgepole pines. She bought the cabin, mining claims and all. And in we moved.

Several months later Max wanted to rip down the poorly-built goat sheds. In one shed, between the top side-wall logs and the roof, he discovered some six-inch cylindrical objects. Max figured he'd better ask Dimp what they could be.

"My God, Max, don't touch 'em," said Dimp. "Them's frozen dynamite." Being an old time miner familiar with dynamite, Dimp man-

34

aged to carefully dispose of them in the river.

Dimp explained to Bestemor and to us about the difference between mining claims and mining patents. "This here is a claim," he said, "and the cabin sets on a mill site. It's called the Des Moines Mill Site. But the mine is the Alhambra Mine. If you look way up above the rockslide along the left hand side of Porcupine Mountain you can see the portal. Ain't much of a portal and I don't rightly know if anyone has worked it. But, you'll have to do $100 a year assessment work on the mine and the mill site to keep 'em. Otherwise someone'll jump your claim. You might try going for a patent. I'll explain all about that some other time."

Evidently the old couple who sold the place to Bestemor weren't interested in mining. They kept goats in all those low connecting sheds. Dimp told us the place was known as the "Goat Ranch" or "Cold Springs" or just the "Alhambra Mine Place." Quite a choice, but soon we were calling it "The Alhambra."

We had a couple of weeks of golden weather. We would have some income as Max had the job of building a mining road for Dimp and his small mining company. The road was to the Hunkidori Mine up above the old ghost town of Saints John.

Rather than stay in the cabin on those beautiful days, I would pile the children in the car and drive up to Montezuma. What a lovely setting for all the old buildings still in use up there. There were two quite large hotels, three stories each, but the white paint on them was so old they looked gray. Along both sides of the dirt road, which was the main street, were several false-fronted buildings, one a pool hall. A little way above the town sat a prim, pristine white schoolhouse with steeple and bell. Perched up there it looked like a stern school teacher looking down over the town and the log cabins scattered among the spruce and on the green grassy hillsides.

In every direction one could see the high peaks already dusted with snow. I had never seen so many golden aspens, entire mountainsides so aflame that they seemed to be lighted from within. The thin air was crisp and cold except when we stood in the warm sunshine.

35

I walked with Rolf and Sunni along narrow mining roads. We rested on a knoll near a fallen-down cabin at a huge mining dump. Silence was everywhere. Walking on farther we came upon a small working mine where the squeak of machinery could be heard. Wood smoke from the cabins in the town would drift up the valley and mingle with the pungent smell of the mineral earth warmed by the sun. I showed the children how to crush juniper berries for another tantalizing odor. "When Bestemor was a young girl in Norway," I told them, "she used to make juniper ale for Christmas from the berries."

One morning we awakened to a dark sky. Snow was whistling by our small cabin. Shortly after breakfast Dimp drove up in his battered red pickup. Coming in and stomping the snow off his boots, he said, "Well

Max, guess mining will have to wait 'til spring so bring your cat down off the mountain." Backing up to warm himself at the open oven door, he stated, "Then we'll start cutting firewood. You haven't got half enough wood. You'll need a sight more to get through the winter. This is a darn good little cook stove, but it'll sure eat up the wood."

"Just how long does winter last here in the Montezuma Valley and Dillon?" I asked Dimp. "We—ll," he looked at me seriously, "if summer comes on a Sunday round here, we have a baseball game."

Max laughed. "Guess we'd better get in more wood then."

I looked at my shiny black "Home Comfort" cook stove standing in the corner of the kitchen. "Home Comfort" was on the two upper warming oven doors and again in raised letters of cast iron on the small front door where I'd shove in the aspen logs. Well named little stove, I decided.

4

High Country Winter

November came. The snowstorm had left only six inches but it was enough for sledding on the hill back of the cabin. The kids had their end-of-the-season rides on their bucking barrel bronc that Max had rigged up. By taking an old oil drum and stringing two ropes through the ends, and tying these ropes to four trees, he could pull the drum up to the height of a small horse. Then, by working the ropes, he could make the barrel go up and down and really buck. With an old saddle we found in the barn tied to the barrel, the kids could sit astride this contraption. They loved riding their horse and waving their cowboy hats in the air.

Saturday was our weekly bath night. Heating all that water on the cookstove more often was just too much work. In between we had "spit baths." We had purchased a big wash tub which we put in the middle of the kitchen floor. I carried in buckets of water to heat and fill the tub. The first bath I thought I'd make really good so I filled the tub to the brim planning to bathe both children at once. Forgetting about displacement, I lifted Sunni in first. The water poured over the sides and I went flying on the linoleum floor, landing on my behind in front of the door. Everytime I would try to get up, I would slide around some more. Rolf, sitting on a chair, was convulsed with laughter at my predicament. Max, hearing all the hilarity, came in from the bedroom and luckily got the mop and mopped up the floor. The floor was never cleaner but I was the one who really needed a bath after that.

By clearing a section of the hillside up the mountain, Max built a slalom slope and a ski jump, with his cat. We packed the inrun and the landing. He could jump 75 feet on it, but I was content with one jump of 25 feet. I had never jumped before and have never done so since. It was exhilarating. Max instructed me, "Pretend you are an eagle and you are descending on your prey as your feet hit the ground." It worked and neither of us fell.

One day Max took the cat down to our homestead, that would some-day become Ski Tip Ranch, to push some of the junk together and bury it. A cowboy came riding by on a beautiful palomino. He introduced himself as Frank Byers and told Max he had a ranch about six miles to the west and a bit north of Dillon. Some of his cattle had strayed and he was trying to locate them. Seeing Max's cat he asked if Max would be willing to do some bulldozing for him. "Come on to dinner tomorrow night and bring your family," Frank told Max. We were so happy to have the chance to meet a ranch family.

What a great family the Byers were. Their ranch had a sweeping view over the meadows to the entire Gore Wilderness Range. Their two daughters were in high school. Mrs. Byers told me it wasn't always easy to get them to school because they had to drive through big snow drifts in winter. I had never heard of school buses then. None of us had an inkling that the big Dillon Dam would one day make of the Byers' meadows a beautiful lake, one of the most dramatic sailing lakes in the high country.

At the cabin our only reading light, in fact our only light, was a kerosene lamp. In order to see what was cooking or to see to stir the gravy on the stove in the dark corner of the kitchen, I would have to hold the lamp over the stove. Seeing me do this, Max said, "This is too dangerous. We'd better go 'over the hill to Ideeho Springs' (quoting Dimp) and see if there's a better and safer light we can buy. Also, Christmas is coming and we need candles for the tree." Over Loveland Pass we went.

At Idaho Springs we found a store which sold anything a miner, or housewife, needed. There we were told that Coleman lanterns gave better light and could hang from the ceiling. We bought two of these. Also, there were the old Christmas tree candles I remembered from my childhood.

But how to fasten them to the branches? Digging around on a long wooden table of miscellaneous items in the back of the store we found some soft pliable wire with which we could fasten the candles to the tree. It was a wonderful feeling that all these long-used old things seemed new to us, a feeling of discovery of things forgotten. Just a few months before we had been living in a modern house on a city street. And here we were thrilled to find this invention, a Coleman gas lantern.

Thanksgiving came, which we shared with Dimp and Lula, but not much more snow. We had heard of Loveland Ski Area on the east side of Loveland Pass. One day we checked it out, but there was only a short rope tow, no T-bars or chair lifts. Crossing the 12,000-foot pass, plus paying for tow tickets, made us decide to stay home until more snow came.

Christmas was a short week away. Max found a small spruce which he "planted" in the snow outside our kitchen window. While I would read to the children in their bedroom before supper, Max would quietly go outside and light the candles on the tree. We didn't dare have the tree indoors with the fire hazard of those candles. After being called to supper the children would discover the lighted tree by themselves and call to us, "Come see what Santa's elves have done. They've lighted the tree again." It was a great Christmas. Then the heavy snows came. It snowed for a whole week. Our little cabin was soon well-insulated.

After the storm I looked out of the window one morning to see Max on his skis packing the snow in front of our cabin. He packed the snow tightly. I couldn't figure out what he was doing until he came in for lunch and announced, "I'm going to build an igloo." The packed snow set up quite hard and by cutting it into blocks and stacking them an igloo soon took shape. He built a bench of snow blocks in the back of the main room. He had found in the barn a pot-bellied wood stove which he put in the middle of the room with the chimney sticking up through the rounded roof. To enter one had to bend over slightly in order to get through the tunnel entrance he'd built in front. In the barn he had also found an old buffalo fur coat. By carefully cutting this, he made a cover for the bench in the igloo. From the leftover fur he made a pair of cowboy chaps to fit Rolf.

40

The children had the most marvelous playhouse. Sunlight filtered through the snow diffusing the whole room with blue and rosy light. The kids would crawl out of the igloo, play in the snow and sun, and then crawl back into the main igloo room to get warm. Adults could even stand up in the main room.

Old Dimp drove up one afternoon and almost ran off the road. "Ain't the cabin big enough for you?" We all laughed. "This is a good time to christen the new addition," I said. I brewed up some hot buttered rum and we sat in the rosy glow of the igloo getting a bit of rosy glow within us. Dimp balanced his drink on his knee and said, "Now is as good a time as any to tell you of a cold night one summer when I coulda used some of this brew." We all settled back on the buffalo fur couch to hear his story.

"It was a moonlit night," Dimp began. "I had the dray wagon business in Dillon then and used to haul freight from Kremmlin' to Dillon. Sometimes I'd haul all the way from Craig and Steamboat Springs. Since it was over Rabbit Ears Pass it'd take two to three days. But this time I'm tellin' of was only up Peru Creek to the Pennsylvania Mine up there."

"Well, the phone rang one night about midnight. There had been an accident at the Pennsylvania Mine and a man had been killed. They wanted to know if I could come right away and bring the body back to Dillon. The mill and mine called the Pennsylvania was a big operation in the early 1900s and they'd had a telephone line strung all the way from Dillon.

"Lula didn't want me to go alone so she dressed in warm clothes and went along. It was a dark cold ride bouncing along on the old Keystone and Montezuma roads and up the winding rutted Peru Creek road to the mine. When we arrived at the mill the full moon came out over Argentine Mountain. The miners were standin' around and they weren't talkin'. You know how it is late at night like that. They were silhouetted against the moonlight but their shadows were long and real black on the ground. It was real spooky.

"After helpin' me load the stiff body onto the flatbed of the dray wagon they watched silently as we started the long ride home. With the clear moonlight it was easier to see the road. The horse went on at a good clip since the grade was a nice gradual downhill. The boys up there had passed around a bottle so Lula and me were feelin' more cheerful and we sang some good old songs. Well, we reached the corner of Montezuma and Keystone roads when Lula looks back. 'The wagon's empty, Dimp,' she yells at me. 'The body's gone!'"

"Well," Dimp continued, "turn around we did fer we had to start the long trip back, hopin' the body hadn't bounced off too far back. Finally, part-way up Peru Creek road on the curves we found the body. It had jolted itself right offen that wagon!"

In Idaho Springs we had found two pair of wooden skis short enough for Rolf and Sunni. But there were no bindings and nowhere to find or buy any. With rubber strips from old inner tubing Max made the

42

bindings. Ski boots for children were unheard of. We'd have to think of something. They did have good rubber overshoes and plenty of wool socks. By wearing the socks inside their shoes, then another pair of socks over the shoes, and then the rubber boots, their feet could stay warm and dry. Strapping on the little skis they would play in the snow, crawling, sliding, climbing and running. Soon they were unaware they had the skis on and could play and slide with no trouble. But *where* could we all go skiing?

In early January we had a surprise visit from a young man who had been on Max's Penn State Ski Team before the war. He was Max Peters and he had just returned from Italy where with the 10th Mountain Division he had been a member of the U.S. Ski Troops. Before going back to Penn State, he wanted to revisit Camp Hale, where he had trained. We all piled into our convertible and took off for Cooper Hill and Camp Hale, both of which we had never seen, but had heard so much about during the war.

Cooper Hill was quite a disappointment because the hill was so short. It seemed like one turn and we were at the bottom. We took turns staying with the children at the base of the lift so they wouldn't get lost. We decided it would be fun to have dinner in historic Leadville at the old Vendome Hotel. When they were training at Camp Hale the ski troopers would come into Leadville for excitement. From what Max Peters told us there was plenty of that in the old mining town.

On the way back home we reached the big brightly-lighted mining operation of Climax on Fremont Pass. The 600-foot ski hill across the road from the mine was well lit, showing the beautiful unmarked powder snow.

Since it was already dark and the youngsters were getting sleepy, we tucked them into the two down sleeping bags we always kept in the back of the car. Clamping on our skis we climbed up to the warming hut. Here we found the reason for the untracked snow. The skiers standing around the pot-bellied stove told us the rope tow would soon start. They only operated for the families at Climax on Wednesday nights and all day Saturday and Sunday. This was a Wednesday and it had snowed soft new powder on Monday and Tuesday. We were welcome to join them and to come on over again whenever we wished.

We skied until 10 o'clock. It was heavenly although my arms ached from the rope tow. It was an unreal world with the exhilaration of floating through all that light powder, in and out of the tree shadows. Below and across the valley bluish-green flares of the Climax Mine lighted the night sky. We could hear dynamite blasts from the mine every now and then. On the way home I told Max and Max that I felt like I was going like hell and probably headed there too. What added to the feeling was the music. Someone had placed loudspeakers on the rope tow poles. They were playing Grieg's *Peer Gynt Suite* and *The Hall of the Mountain King* was especially appropriate.

An hour later found us tired but happy at home in the little cabin. Where to put our guest? In the kitchen, of course, on the folding army cot. Any good ski trooper had his own sleeping bag.

The next morning Max and Max decided to explore an area they had heard was a tremendous alpine-type bowl. Where they went, I had no idea. I heard Max tell Max Peters that if you looked south from the top of Loveland Pass you could look right into this area.

Late in the afternoon they returned and over supper described their trip. "It's like the open slopes of the Alps in Switzerland."

"We came upon two old log cabins. That means there must have been some mining up in there."

The next day Max Peters had to leave. I wondered if we'd ever see him again. Years later he became Dean of Colorado University's School of Engineering. Each winter we see him at all the Veteran's ski races. Over a beer, after the day's race, we sit down and reminisce of that powder snow evening at Climax.

Max seemed very quiet the rest of the day. I finally asked him if something was worrying him. "No," he said, "but I've been thinking of those two cabins up in that high alpine meadow. We almost missed them because they were so covered with snow. If Max hadn't sailed off the roof of one of them, we might not have seen them at all. What I think I'll do is find out about them before the County Commissioners meet. Dimp told

44

me that if taxes haven't been paid on old mining patents, you can bid on them. On second thought, maybe I'd better go to the Court House tomorrow and see if they are patented. The treasurer would know since patented mines are taxed."

This all seemed bewildering to me. "Why on earth, Max," I asked "do you want to acquire some old cabins way up where you have to ski tour so far to get to them?"

Max laughed, "It's not the cabins I'm interested in, honey."

"Well, why then?" I questioned.

"The fact is that there might be a millsite and some mines up there. Remember when I worked for the Forest Service back in '42? I got to know and like a Forest Service ranger at the Idaho Springs office, a fellow named Slim Davis. He told me that the best possible future ski area around was that alpine bowl up there. I've been looking at it every time we go over Loveland Pass. And after all that Dimp has told me about claims and patents, I'm just curious."

Back in October Max started to grow a beard. By Janaury it was quite full and curly which was helpful when he arrived at the Court House. He was thought to be just another miner in from the hills. Commissioners met only the first Monday of the month so we had to wait until February. In the meantime Max had found out that the millsite, which included five acres and the mines up there, were all on the delinquent tax roll.

February came, and the Commissioners' meeting. Happily for us they accepted Max's bid. We learned we would have to wait a month until they had advertised our bid every week in the local Summit County Journal. No one came forward to raise the bid, and March 1st found us the owners of land in this beautiful snow bowl.

In the meantime we had heard of a race in early March on Loveland Pass at what was known as the "Mine Dump." I hadn't raced since the Pennsylvania State Championships. The thought of our entering downhill and slalom races near Loveland Pass was exciting. Bestemor had come up from Boulder to be with us, so we had a baby sitter.

Max's beard was quite a novelty at the starting gate. Nobody wore beards then so there was general kidding. "Here's the man from Mars."

45

Summer

Rolf Dercum

The warm humming
of a summer morning
in the beaver meadows
bright with light and color
So pervasively green
in contrast to
the earth colors of spring

That almost all memory
of these colors
is forgotten
Everything is immediate

"What tree have you been living under?" "The Original Mountain Man."

The downhill was a disaster for me. I fell hard and sprained my ankle. The next morning I had to be content to be a spectator. Before the race started the racers stood around making comments and waxing their skis. One of the racers turned around and pointed into our snow bowl. "Over there is where we are going to have this race next year." Max looked at me and I looked at him and he nodded at me. I realized that was where Max bought our mining patents.

After the race we found the racer who had made that remark. His name was Larry Jump. He called his friend Sandy Schauffler to meet us. Sandy had been the starter for the race. Larry explained to us that he and Sandy had been hired by the state to look into possible areas for ski development. Finding out that we owned the only private land in the bowl, which they called "Arapahoe Basin," they asked if they could come down the next week and talk with us. We told them, "Any day but Saturday or Sunday. We are over at Climax those days."

It was early one morning in March, a sunny morning and we were having a leisurely breakfast in the kitchen. Looking out the window to the west, I said to Max, "Remember when Dimp and Lula told us of how Mr. Sheard, who sold this cabin to Bestemor, saw a bear standing out there right under the clothesline. He opened the window and shot the bear. That was in March. Guess we'd better keep an eye on Sunni and Rolf when they're playing outside." As I was looking out the window and thinking about seeing a bear out there, I saw a car come up the road. We didn't see many cars on Montezuma road. Usually the only ones were the mailman or Dimp and Lula who would come roaring up in their red pickup to check on us. But this was a car we'd not seen before and it slowed and then turned in at our mailbox.

We were all of us still in our pajamas. While Max rapidly changed into his jeans, I grabbed the children and tore into the bedroom to change. From the bedroom window I could see three men get out of the car and slowly walk toward our very unprepossessing cabin. "Why Max, it's Larry Jump and Sandy Schauffler and another man. Oh Lord, the kitchen's a mess." Max was already greeting them at the door and inviting

46

them in. By the time I got myself and the children dressed they were already sitting at the kitchen table. Max had shoved the dishes to one side and was pouring coffee for the men.

The third man was Thor Groswold. "My skis are Groswold skis," I exclaimed. "Yes, that's my company," he answered. "I understand you are Norwegian too." He was so tall that I hurriedly asked him to sit down again before he hit his head on our low ceiling.

I didn't think they would stay too long but they talked and talked. Finally, it was afternoon. I hadn't been able to clear the table at all, but they didn't seem to mind. I took the children for a walk up the road, apprehensive that maybe a bear might amble along and meet us. The men were just beginning to leave when we returned and one of them said "Well, we have us a corporation." The Arapahoe Basin Corporation was founded that day at our table, loaded with dirty dishes, in the little Alhambra cabin.

Spring was coming and time to start work on our new home-to-be down the road. We had had much fun skiing each weekend at Climax and meeting that great family, the Gorsuches. Jack and Zella had three children, David, Bill and Jackie. Bill was just finishing high school and Jackie was at Western State at Gunnison. Seven-year-old David skied all over the hill with a wide snowplow, much to the admiration of our three- and four-year-olds. Next winter, David really slapped his skis together. It wasn't long before he was one of the top junior racers in the U.S. Fourteen years later he was one of the top U.S. racers in the 1960 Winter Olympics games at Squaw Valley. Jack and Zella were untiring in their work and encouragement at the Climax hill. All season they were setting slalom courses, gate keeping, or standing all day at the finish line in cold or freezing weather with a stop watch. They were often helping load the kids on the rope tow or T-bar or keeping the pot-bellied stove going in the small warming shelter. No wonder so many well-known racers came from that area. We were always welcome to spend Saturday nights at their home so we wouldn't have to drive the 30 miles back to our little cabin.

5

Spring Muck Out

The snow was beginning to melt around the cabin, but we still had flurries. Winter hated to let go. We had heard of cabin fever, but so far had not been affected by it. However, one day Bestemor suggested that Max and I should take a trip down to Denver for a change of scene. "The grass is probably already green down dere," she said. That was all I needed.

"I can take care of the children," Bestemor offered, "and maybe teach them how to make Norwegian lefsa." Welcoming her fine offer, we decided to try it for one day and a night.

One day and one night was enough in the city. I already missed seeing the children playing around the cabin in their bulky, roly-poly clothes, looking like a couple of little bear cubs themselves.

Arriving home, we found all was fine except that Bestemor was a bit upset by something which had happened in the night. She was about to fall asleep when she heard stomping around on the roof of the cabin just over her head. She guessed that some kids from Dillon, joy-riding around, had decided to have fun and climb the roof of the cabin. She knew this could be easily done since the roof on the north side slanted almost to the ground. Taking a flashlight, she went out the front door on the south side but she could see nothing. Waving the flashlight around, she called out, "You yust get off of dere." Total silence. She went back into the cabin, waited for a while, and then fell sound asleep.

Max and I were puzzled because she said she hadn't seen any car. We

48

went around to the back of the cabin. There were huge bear paw tracks in the snow on the roof!

We discovered that the original main cabin at our ranch was built in 1869. After getting all the flowery wallpaper off, plus the rotted brown cheesecloth glued to the handhewn logs, Max found newspapers stuffed into the cracks between the logs and some nailed to the walls. One of these he gingerly peeled off. It was brittle and brown with age and mouse droppings. He was amazed to discover it was a London paper dated 1869.

Cleaning that cabin was something. Max had a dust-filtering mask which the "cat skinners" in the Pacific Northwest use when they are logging in the dry and dusty season. I also really needed it. With a fervor to really get down to the logs, I attacked the old wallpaper. Max had given me a rake with sharp points so I could tear into the paper and cheesecloth. It was quite an operation. I took the rake and with a swing at the Arabian-tent-like ceiling, I ripped through the wallpaper. The cheesecloth had first been tacked from joist to joist. Then the wallpaper had been glued to it.

Due to many years of either affluence, when the mines paid off or the overnight guests at this stagecoach stop could afford the rates, or years of scanty income, we found the story of their good or lean days. First there were layers of gilded paper, then rather ordinary paper, then layers of newspaper. Along the walls in the two upper loft rooms we found that they had resorted to stuffing the cracks with bright pink, worn-out silk underwear. Covering all this to keep out the cold drafts, the walls were lined with cardboard cartons opened up and nailed to the logs. Some of these even had the name of the grocery store still in existence in Dillon, "Sondregger's Grocery," which my good friend, Irma Feaster, had been leasing back in that summer of '42.

With my rake I took my first hearty swipe at the ceiling. Down came a big swath of paper and dust. I fled outside into the bright sun until the dust settled. Max had a big bonfire started so I could shovel all the "muck," as the miners called it, on the fire.

Using the borrowed Forest Service portable pump and water tank we cleaned the logs with water pressure. I then used a broom and a knife to remove what was left of the old mud chinking.

The first time, after the dust had settled, I went back in. But the sun and snow patches outside had blinded me a bit for the darker room inside. Something hit me in the face! Backing away in alarm, I waited for my eyes to adjust. Then, I saw it. From a single strand of cheese cloth hung the skeleton of a pack rat. This had struck me directly in the face as it swung to and fro. I hit it with my rake. Now I knew what the miners meant when they said, "I gotta muck out my cabin."

Max had brought out from Washington some wire rope he'd used while logging there. He literally "wrapped" these cables around the old log lean-to which was attached to the main house. Using these cables he'd

50

back up the cat and it would all tumble down. Later in the spring we sawed these logs into fireplace lengths. When our fireplace would be built we knew we'd have a good supply of unpeeled logs.

In May we decided we'd better move out of the Alhambra cabin to be nearer our own ranchwork. There was an old two-room cabin near our ranch house beside the road. We had heard from our friends in Longview, Washington, the Ganongs, that they would like to come out to see what Colorado mountain country was like. We wondered where they could stay. Also, Max's mother and father had decided they would like to live near us in Colorado. Adina and Earl Ganong wrote that they had sold their house in Longview. They planned to bring their two children, Eleanor and Joanna, and also Adina's Swedish mother. Our letters must have painted a tempting picture. We had written them there might be a ski area going in, that is if the money could be raised to do the job.

What decided or prompted Max's parents, we weren't quite sure, except Max's mother had fallen in love with Colorado the first time she had seen the high mountain country. They wrote us they had sold their home and would be shipping all their furniture, and for us to keep an eye out for it.

After Bestemor had cleaned out the cabin near the road, we moved in. Bestemor had made many friends in the county. One day she announced that we could let the Ganongs use her Alhambra cabin. She was going "down the Blue" (river) to a ranch to cook for the ranch hands who were irrigating and would later be haying in August. I knew she was looking forward to this because there hadn't been much for her to do at the cabin. Before leaving she had bought us another Home Comfort cook stove for $15.00 which she had found in Idaho Springs. We were all set to welcome the Ganongs. But what about Max's parents?

During the winter we had driven up to Montezuma a few times. There we had seen a very handsome house about a quarter of a mile beyond the town. Max told me that in summer it was used as a boarding house. Years before it had been "the place" to stay when the horse-drawn stage came over Argentine Pass on its way to the mining camps and Dillon. Luckily, for us, we heard that the lady who owned the "White

House," as it was called, was up in Montezuma and had opened for the summer. This solved the problem for the moment of where Max's parents could stay while they arranged for their house to be built. Max's father, an architect, had already drawn up the plans. During the winter he had sent us sketches of their new house. We promised them two acres on which to build somewhere in our meadow. They only had to pick the spot.

The snow begins to melt up in Montezuma.

Early one Sunday morning in May I could hear the sound of a truck coming up the road. We had just moved into the cabin, and being close to the road, we could easily hear any vehicles that passed. The truck started to slow down. It's coming here, I thought. Sure enough, it shifted down and turned into the yard.

We jumped out of bed, dressed in a hurry, and ran outside. The truck driver was getting out of the cab. He looked around at the old two-room

52

cabin and the ranch house with no chinking between the logs. He also noted the open hay shed, the horse barn, chicken coop, and two log vehicle sheds. "I've got a truck load of furniture. Where do you want me to unload it?" he asked. We looked around in complete astonishment.

"Oh my God, my folks have sent all their stuff already! We'll have to put it in the nearest shed," said Max. "I'll have to check to see if it's clean enough." Looking into the shed, we found it had a wood floor of sorts and it was empty. "Why not put it all in there for the time being?" I said. As the furniture was being unloaded I looked at the lovely white-covered couch, the maple ladder-backed chairs, and dining table and the seven-foot high cherry cabinet with original glass-paned windows. Somehow, I couldn't see all this stacked in an old, almost falling-down storage shed. What to do?

During the winter we had met a miner, Max Bunker, who was operating up on Independence Mountain, the mountain rising just south of the ranch. Max Bunker came driving up the road just as all the furniture was being set down on the dirt. It all looked so incongruous with the log cabins as a background. The Dercum home in Cleveland, with all these lovely things, had been featured in *Town & Country Magazine*. Max Bunker looked it all over, then sat down on the couch. "Well, might as well enjoy it now. It won't last long in that cabin with the mice playing tag on the rafters!"

Max Bunker stretched out his legs and with a luxurious sigh, said, "I know a guy who couldn't enjoy sittin' on this comfortable couch for awhile. A couple of nights ago Ike and I drove up Keystone Gulch to visit our friends at a cabin up there.

"They invited us to stay for supper. We sat around chewin' the fat. Ike went back of the cabin to the privy 'fore we left. It bein' dark he stumbled around 'til he found it.

"All of a sudden we heard this god-awful yell. Here came Ike, bustin' into the cabin with his pants down around his knees.

"I sat on a porcupine!" he yells at us.

"Well, we made him lie down on the floor on his face, while the wife holds the kerosene lamp, her husband holds down Ike—and I pulls the

M.D.
'81

54

quills out. Ike ain't gonna be sittin' down fer awhile!''

We spent the day storing the boxed items in the log shed. The rest, along with the oriental rugs, went right into the two-room cabin. Surprisingly, it all fit in.

We invited Max B. for lunch and a beer. Just as we were sitting down, we heard a car drive up. Here were Max's parents! ''We've arrived!'' they exclaimed. ''Didn't expect you so soon,'' I said, wondering what they would say when they saw the furniture in the cabin. But, on entering, they laughed. ''Not a bad home for the time being and it looks cozy. Mother and I will drive up to Montezuma and get settled in that nice boarding house Max told us about. Then we'll see about starting to build.'' Father and Mother Dercum were called ''Opa'' and ''Oma'' by all of us.

We had no more than taken a deep sigh of relief when we heard another car drive up. It was an old Studebaker with a camper-trailer pulled behind. ''Hi! We made it!'' Out climbed Earl and Adina Ganong followed by their two little blond girls, Eleanor and Joanna age five and three. ''Who's that in the back?'' I asked after greetings all around. ''Oh, that's my mom, Mormor. You remember her from Longview?'' ''Of course,'' I answered and went up to the car to welcome her. Now we had a Bestemor and a Mormor, and they'd be company for each other.

''We've brought all our furniture and we sold the Longview house,'' Earl announced. ''We are here to stay.''

''Well, let me show you the Alhambra cabin up the road where we lived last winter,'' said Max. ''Then all of you come back down here and we'll have a cookout to celebrate your arrival. It's great that you all got here the same day. You'll no more'n get settled, Earl, than I'll bet we'll be working up at the mountain cutting ski trails. It's funny, but we'll probably be using the same saw, and it's the same cat and truck we had when we worked together out of Longview last summer.'' Max took off with the Ganong caravan following. I thought, all winter we have had only two neighbors and suddenly we have nine.

55

6

Montezuma, the Alhambra and Arapahoe

The snow began melting in the high country and June finally arrived. Sandy and Larry came up from Denver one day and asked if we could put up six boys and feed them while they worked on the new ski area. They needed Max and his cat for the road building and clearing trails. The boys, all easterners, were teenagers, sons of friends of Larry and Sandy, who might buy stock in the Arapaho Basin Corporation. We were told they were eager to work. The Forest Service permit had come through and everything was set to go. They could ride up to Arapahoe Basin every day with Max and Earl.

There was no furniture in the main ranch house where the boys would sleep, but it was clean. We had scrubbed down the logs using portable fire-fighting equipment for pressure, utilizing water from the small irrigation ditch which ran in front of the house and our cabin. The work crew would be eating in our cabin. They were from Dartmouth, Harvard, and similar colleges. I knew they'd feel right at home using the hardwood ladder-back chairs and table and the white couch. Oma held her breath when she saw these six-footers leaning back on her lovely chairs. Luckily, the chairs were New England-made and survived this rough treatment.

Our biggest problem was feeding the boys, and us, for that matter. We had a little savings and could buy some meat. I had put in a garden back of the old barn and could see the carrots and lettuce coming up. Iceberg lettuce was one of the things which didn't freeze at night. The days were warm but at night it got so cold sometimes there would be a thin sheet of ice on the water bucket. We had put a bench out front with a wash basin and bucket. Towels we hung on nails and there was a cracked mirror on the wall. If the boys wanted to have a bath they could go down to the river, which they did. As one boy said, "That river's so cold I couldn't hang on to the soap."

Meat, vegetables and salad we had. What else to feed these hungry boys? Mormor came to the rescue showing me how to bake six loaves of bread in the wood stove. Six loaves a day it was. Breakfast took some, lunches took a lot. Usually when they returned from the mountain with Max, I had taken the fresh loaves out of the oven. The boys would sit right down and go through a loaf or more before it cooled, spreading butter on so it would melt. Then, they were happy for a couple of hours until supper.

Our little savings fund was slipping away, but we felt it was for a good cause. By mid-July we couldn't afford to buy meat for these hungry boys. Max Bunker appeared one day with half a venison. I asked him, "How come? It's July. This isn't hunting season, Max."

"If them durn Texans can come up here in October and hunt, I guess us locals can go out when it's safe and we won't get shot by them fellows."

He continued, "I gotta apologize for the grass stains on the meat. What happened was, after I shot it and skinned it out, I went back into the mine. A bear got it and started to drag it off. I trailed him and got it back."

Adina and I bought a big pressure cooker and began canning all the venison into stews and sauces. This became necessary as soon we acquired more venison.

One day Dimp came tearing up in his old pickup. He was trembling all over when he got out. It was before supper and Max and Earl and the boys had just pulled in. They walked over to see what was wrong.

Dimp shouted, "I gotta have help. I've got a doe down in front of my barn." Seeing Max and Earl standing there ready to help, he took a deep breath and relaxed. "Lula made me so nervous 'cause I'd never shot a deer before. I saw this doe come up to the barn where my three goats were standin' 'round and she just stood there. So, I rushed up to our bedroom and grabbin' the rifle, lit for the back porch. I took careful aim with Lula hangin' on to me and beggin' 'Don't shoot, Dimp, don't shoot.' I said, Unhand me, woman.' I takes careful aim, but just a click. I'd forgotten to load the damned thing. So, I tears back upstairs, gets the ammunition and loads the gun. Darned if that deer wasn't still standin' there with my goats. I aims careful and hits her."

We all felt sad about it, knowing how Dimp felt, but we knew there was a lot of summer ahead of us and a lot of mouths to feed. Dimp said, as the guys loaded into the truck to go back and help him, "I knew all you folks here needed it and I wanted to help out."

The next day the three of us, Oma, Adina and I were cutting up the venison on the table in our cabin kitchen, the same maple wood table, when there was a knock on the door. The winter before we had met a fellow who was with the High Altitude Observatory at Climax. We became good friends. He was Dr. Walter Orr Roberts, Director of the Observatory.

Here he was at our door and there was someone with him. He introduced the portly and very dignified gentleman as Dr. Harlow Shapley, Director of Harvard University Observatory.

Dr. Shapley looked at Oma Dercum, who was wearing a bloody apron made of flour sacking, her grey hair all askew, at Adina, still cutting away on the meat at the table, and at me, who was just as messy. "Dercum?" he looked puzzled. I guessed he was wondering to himself, 'Roberts, what have you brought me into?' "Dercum?" he said again. "I used to know a Dr. Dercum in Philadelphia, who was President of the American Philosophical Society when I was Vice-President. It can't be the same family, can it?"

Poor Oma. A graduate of Vassar '06, she was accustomed to being out of her "morning clothes" and dressed in the afternoon for any friends who might call at her Shaker Heights, Ohio, home. She looked as if she wanted the floor to open up and swallow her. But, in all her five feet of dignity, she smiled at Dr. Shapley and said, "Dr. Francis X. Dercum was my husband's cousin." To break the awkward moment, Dr. Roberts asked, "Is that hamburger? I like nothing better than good, fresh hamburger." So, we wrapped up some for him.

Father Dercum came in and was introduced. We decided it was coffee break time, moved chairs outdoors on the shady side the cabin, and served them coffee and fresh buttered bread. Oma had quickly washed after running over to the ranch house, where she kept some clean, fresh clothes. It was great fun sitting in the grass or on the stiff-backed chairs, listening to the irrigation ditch dancing along near the garden. Dr. Shapley was telling Father about the great plans for an atmospheric research center to be built at Boulder.

Back at Penn State my 15-year-old nephew, Peter, wanted to come west. He had left home the year before. His desire to become a cowboy led him to New Mexico where his mother soon located him and brought him back home. However, his parents decided that if he was with us in Colorado for the summer, or maybe for the entire year, he might get this desire out of his system.

Following Peter's arrival, a letter came from his dad. Knowing Max had taught Peter calf roping and how to ride a horse when we were back at Penn State, his dad felt that we should be fully responsible for the boy since we had enticed him out west. I took Peter aside and asked him to be really careful and not do anything dangerous. He smiled at me and said, "Don't worry, Aunt Edna, I know how to take care of myself." Then I *really* felt worried.

All the boys working at Arapahoe Basin, plus Peter, were eagerly looking forward to the local rodeo. None of us, except Max who had worked on ranches in Montana and the Dakota Badlands, had seen a rodeo. It was a beautiful Sunday in July. The corral was just north of Dillon. There were no bleachers. We all sat on the fence or on the hoods of the cars parked behind the fence. There was a cool breeze from the mountain snow fields mingling with the smell of dust and sage being trampled by the milling horses.

We all stood in the dust while the American anthem was being sung over the loudspeaker. I was enjoying it all: the parade on horseback with flags flying; the bucking horses throwing off their riders; and the calf roping. Everything was festive with the children excited and stuffing themselves with hot dogs prepared by the 4-H Club.

I wondered where Max was, and couldn't see him or Peter anywhere. They're probably checking out the horses, I thought.

"Look, Rolf and Sunni," I exclaimed, "There's a clown! Isn't he funny? Look at his big red nose and those black and white striped overalls with the crotch down to his knees. And all that red hair. He's got a rope and he's trying to catch a calf." Somebody nearby yelled, "Look, he caught the calf. That's better than most of the riders have done."

60

On the other side of the corral a man had fallen off the fence and was running over to the clown. "Hey!" the man yelled to the clown. "You've dropped your whiskey flask and it's all runnin' out in the dirt." The clown picked up the flask just as the man made a desperate dive into the dirt to try and grab it. The crowd roared with laughter. I thought, what a different 4th of July!

Balancing myself on the top unpeeled log pole of the fence, uncomfortable as it was, I was enjoying it all when I heard over the loudspeaker, "The steer ridin' is next, folks. Hang onto your hats. Comin' out of the chute is Pete DeJuhasz on steer number five." My God, I said to myself, I never dreamed he'd do this after my warning. I could just see him going head over, being trampled, breaking ribs, arms, legs and collar bones. All we needed is Peter in the hospital.

However, ride that steer Peter did, and he won the first prize money. At the end of the day Peter came swaggering over to us with a big smile. "Well, Aunt Edna, you won't have to feed me anymore. I've got a job as a cowboy out at the Higgins' Hidden Valley Ranch for the summer. Come on over and meet 'em. You'll really like 'em." And we did. It was at the Higgins ranch, during a branding party that started at 7 a.m., where I tasted my first prairie (or Rocky Mountain) oysters. Max horrified me later when he explained to me that these "oysters" are removed when bull calves are made into steers!

It was surprising to me when someone would drive in from Penn State. Some we scarcely knew. I think it was curiousity that directed them to see how we fared out here in the "wild west."

One such couple arrived, friends of Peter's family, when I was in the middle of my laundry. I had to haul the water in buckets and heat it on the stove. Then I scrubbed the dirty socks, jeans, towels and other laundry using an old fashioned scrubbing board in the tub. Our visitors were checking up on us, I thought.

Quickly I covered the tub of soapy water with the clothes soaking in it, and asked them to sit down while I fixed some coffee. "We thought we'd stay over 'til tomorrow night if it's O.K. with you," they said. "Sure," I said, as I frantically thought, where will I put them? Then I remembered we had put up twin beds in the loft room above where the six boys were staying in the ranch house. I had enough clean bedding, so made up the beds. I showed them where they could wash outside. Also the three-seater privy out under the aspen trees.

When they were all set I told them, "We are invited to a bridge and pot luck party this evening. I know you'll be more than welcome. It's Saturday and the boys working at the ski area like to go to Denver for the weekend. I don't have to worry about feeding them." I sat around talking to the couple who looked amazedly around them. "Don't you get terribly bored out here?" asked the wife. I thought to myself, I'm bored *right now.*

I would rather have had my clothes drying in the wind and been off on a walk with the children. They, thankfully, were up at Ganongs playing cowboys and Indians around the cliffs of Porcupine Mountain. Instead I had to sit here and serve tea to someone I'd never visited or had them visit us back east. We had never wanted to belong to the country club crowd of which they were active members. Max, Earl and the boys finally came back.

After washing up, changing clothes and gathering the kids from up the road, we headed out to one of the ranches for a delicious dinner and several hours of bridge. Fortunately, our "guests" were bridge players *par excellence,* so Max and I, who were complete beginners, bowed out and enjoyed kibitizing.

About 10 o'clock someone said, "It's time to get over to the Dillon Town Hall for the dance." I told our guests that it would be a lively square dance and a potluck supper.

"You'll be right hungry after a square or two," they were informed by a player at their table.

"We've never done any square dancing," they said beseechingly.

"Oh, we'll learn you," one of our good rancher friends assured them.

I think it was about 3 o'clock in the morning when our Mr. Guest

62

asked, with his eyes about to close, "When does this ordeal by dance end?" We took pity on them and drove home. I didn't have the heart to tell them that they would be awakened at 6 o'clock the next morning so we could all be out at the Higgins ranch for the branding. We were looking forward to it: the beer cooling in the stream; trying to hold down a young calf (which I was determined to try and did); and the great supper on the ranch house porch overlooking the valley to the Ten Mile Range.

The next morning, as our guests took their departure, I noticed they did not ask me if we ever got bored out here. Mrs. Guest did say, with a twinkle in her eyes, "Can't wait to tell my friends back east about those prairie oysters." I said, "I didn't tell you, because he didn't want me to, but Tom Higgins, our host at the branding yesterday, is a graduate of Penn State and his wife is a graduate of Wells College. Out here we couldn't have better neighbors. Frankly, I don't care where they come from and what's more, they don't care where we come from." "It's another world," she said as they drove off, and I thought, thank God.

Now Interstate I-70 intersects Hidden Valley Ranch. Condominiums start long before you come to the ranch house site. As I drive down from the Eisenhower Tunnel today, I look to the right when I come to the lovely green meadows and think back to those branding parties at the Higgins ranch. Luckily, no condos have been built on those meadows, only across the highway to the south. Peter went back years later. He found the old garden gate and part of the "hoopie" they would ride backwards to town. A hoopie is an old car which has been modified so it drives backwards to push hay in the fields.

Dimp and Lula knew I wanted a "real bath tub." Here they came one day with a big oil drum in the back of their pickup. It had been slit down the long side and halfway across the ends. These flaps had been folded back. Then they lifted it out of the truck onto the ground. The folded-out sides set right into the dirt so it was very steady. "There," said Dimp, "you've got the best goldarned bathtub in the county. All you gotta do is fill it from the ditch in the morning. Let the water warm in the sun and you've got a real nice bath." How great, I thought, and thanked them heartily.

"By the way, Dimp," I asked, "do you know who that clown was at the rodeo Sunday?" Dimp and Lula laughed loudly. Lula just about choked she laughed so hard.

"You mean you don't know? Why, you eat breakfast with him every day and even sleep with him."

"What?" I couldn't believe it. Max? But, then again, who else could have caught that calf? Max had even tried to teach me some rope tricks. "Of course, he didn't dare tell us. He probably thought Oma and Opa and I, too, would be upset. Wait till I tell him I know."

"Don't be too hard on him, Edna," said Dimp. "After all, I loaned him those striped overalls. A cowboy wouldn't be caught dead in that kind, but I wear 'em in the mine."

When the crew returned that afternoon from Arapahoe Basin, I asked Max, "By the way, I've been wondering who that clown was at the rodeo last Sunday?"

"You're looking right at him, honey," Max smiled. "But don't tell Oma and Opa. They'll think I've really come down in the world."

"That flask of whiskey you had in your back pocket, where did you get that?" I asked.

"It was funny when that old cowboy dove for it in the dust. I let it fall out on purpose to see what would happen. It looked like whiskey was flowing out of it, but Lula had filled it only with tea. She and Dimp thought up that one."

"Come over here and see the beautiful bathtub that Lula and Dimp brought."

"It'll take a lot of buckets of water from the irrigation ditch to fill it," Max said.

"I can already envision myself lying luxuriously in all that sun warmed water," I answered. I decided that first thing tomorrow I would try it.

Next morning found me hauling buckets of water to fill the tub. I'd set it up on the east side of the cabin where it would get the early morning sun and none of the afternoon west wind. One drawback was that this was close to the Montezuma Road with no trees for privacy. I

64

remembered that in the shed, stored with Oma and Opa's other items, was a four-paneled wooden folding screen. If I put this around the head of the tub I would be well-shielded from any cars going by on the road.

After lunch when the kids were taking their naps I undressed in the cabin. I wrapped the towel around me and ran out to the tub. Draping the towel over the screen, I climbed into this delicious warm water and stretched out full length. It was a good sized oil drum. Soaping myself, I let the water run over my arms outstretched to the sun. I listened to the birds, the ripple of ditch water running past the garden, the chattering of chipmunks, and thought, what luxury.

Suddenly, although I was not aware of the arrival of a car, I heard someone laughing and the gentle tooting of a car horn. I looked around.

There was a car parked at the gate with two couples watching me and laughing hilariously. Bewildered, I looked for the screen. The breeze had blown it gently over and there in the dust lay both the screen and the towel. Embarrassed, I ducked down as far as I could into the tub. Fortunately they took pity on me and soon drove away. I made a wild dash to the cabin. After that I had Max move the tub so the cabin was between me and the road.

I had seen pictures of peasants washing clothes at the side of a stream. It was too warm to wear a "babushka" on my head, but I felt that I should do so to make the picture perfect. With my tub of warmed water set down next to the irrigation ditch, and with a scrubbing board I'd found in Dillon, I could do the laundry, rinsing it all in the ditch.

Our garden was doing well as far as lettuce and carrots were concerned. The peas were starting to develop too. Soon the boys would have something besides lettuce and carrots every night. We had used up all of our canned salmon from Washington, but it had helped to vary our venison diet.

After supper was finished, I would take any leftovers out to my compost heap near the garden. In order to get to the garden, I had to jump the irrigation ditch. One evening as I jumped across, I almost collided with a startled fawn. She had been nibbling at my lettuce. She stopped in fright and I did too, but not in fright. I was so thrilled to be within touching distance of this beautiful animal. We stared at each other for several seconds in the bright moonlight. Suddenly she whirled around and literally flew into the aspens. I threw my arms up to the moon and laughed. "I love it here," I shouted. No one heard me but the fawn which was watching from the shadows of the aspens.

Rolf and Sunni and the Ganong children climbed and played on the slopes of the mountains. They would come home each day with a tick or two buried in their hair. Dimp and Lula had warned us to check not only the children, but ourselves. Since all of the children were fair haired, it was no problem to find these dark slow-crawling insects. At first I was terrified at the thought of their getting tick fever with a doctor no nearer than Idaho Springs. Fortunately they stayed well. Max worked hard clearing out the nearby dead timber. After getting rid of the old buildings, building two ponds, and irrigating our meadow, we hardly saw any more ticks.

The Arapahoe Basin Corporation didn't have much money. Luckily, Max, Earl and the six boys working up there did not require much pay. Max used his bulldozer, and charged enough to keep it going. Our savings were dwindling because of the high grocery bills. The old cabin up in the alpine meadow in the Basin was in good shape. I suggested to Larry and Sandy that I loan them a cook stove. Bestemor had found another one in Idaho Springs for ten dollars. If they could find a cook, the boys could bunk up there. Sometime later a fellow from Texas came up to cook, and the boys moved up to Arapahoe Basin. Thank heavens.

The chairlift line had been cut and cleared up the mountain and two trails were ready. A small shelter of lumber and slabs, designed by Opa, was in the process of being constructed at Midway next to the unloading platform site for the lower lift. A track cable was needed for the lift. Someone knew of a used mining cable which could be bought for much less than a new one. The mine, where the cable was bought, was somewhere near Monarch Pass. Max tells about getting the cable:

> It was a rough old drive up this crooked shelf road full of switchbacks and just wide enough for the flatbed truck. A half mile up there, at about 11,000 feet, was a diesel "cat" coughing away. The "cat-skinner" pointed out a kind of ramp where a tremendous reel, wound with about a mile of one-and-a-quarter-inch steel cable, sat ready to load.
>
> After a lot of pushing and pulling with the dozer, we finally got the monster loaded on the truck. Somehow we avoided giving the one wrong nudge which could have sent the whole outfit screaming into the South Fork of the Arkansas River 1,000 feet below.

Soon we would see this cable, which for years had trammed tons of silver ore off a rugged mountain, serve as a track for moving thousands of skiers up into the silvery snow fields high on Norway Mountain.

With September came the turning of the aspens and cold nights. We had finished with all the canning and were ready for winter to come. Oma and Opa had been working on their house down in our meadow. They were lucky to have found three Swedes at the old Keystone village. The village was not a village but merely a few old cabins, a couple of neat newer cabins, and a house of board and batten painted white. There was a sawmill to the west of Keystone where these Swedes had been working.

Opa had been upset when he received the first load of lumber from the sawmill up in Montezuma. Sometimes there would be a difference in width of 1 to 1¾ inch of the boards. Pete Liden, John Flinkberg, or Erick Erickson would look at a board, then take an axe or hatchet and start trimming. When they had finished that board would measure perfectly from top to bottom.

With the scarcity of materials so soon after the war, it looked like the house couldn't be finished until spring. Driving that dusty road, where Opa had counted 28 curves, up to Montezuma to the boarding house would be too much come winter. It was decided that the old main cabin would be comfortable for us. Besides the two good-sized rooms downstairs, there was a narrow stairway along the side of the hall which separated the rooms. This led to two loft rooms upstairs which could be our bedrooms. We located another cookstove for the kitchen, and a pot-bellied stove for the other room which would be the living room. I began to feel quite elegant with all these rooms. The hand hewn squared-timber walls we had oiled. With new plaster chinking I thought it looked beautiful. It still does 35 years later.

Oma and Opa moved into the little cabin feeling very much at home with all their furniture finally theirs to use again. We were all set to hole up again for another winter. But we still had no electricity.

Since we'd used all of our savings to feed the crew during the summer we were glad Max had a job for the winter. Money was still needed to put in the lifts. A rope tow had been installed on the hill above the Mid-

"Is this the place, Max? The Lenawee millsite?"

My first glorious day in Arapahoe Basin—January 1946

The new Arapahoe Basin Corporation and friends Jack & Hank, Memorial Day—1946. (left to right: Earl Ganong, Edna, Max, Sandy Schauffler, Jack Gorsuch, Larry Jump, Adina Ganong, Dick Durrance. Hank the Pilot)

*Max in his element—
early morning
powder.*

*"The Valley of the
Snake"
Ski Tip Ranch in
center of photo, left
of Montezuma
Road, includes big-
gest bend of the
river at foot of
Keystone Mountain.*

70

way meadow not too far from the shelter. The crew had built nearby a three-seater privy on a knoll among the spruce. I was told that if you were quite sure no one would be coming by, you could leave the door open and enjoy a spectacular view of Black Mountain. However, I never trusted my luck that much.

Earl thought the privy was a bit cold for the customers. He found some old fur somewhere and lined the edges of the privy seats. He said it was probably the only ski area with the distinction of having mink-lined toilet seats.

Publicity was needed. There had been one or two small articles in the Denver papers of the "fabulous" new ski area to be opened in the winter of 1946. But not much else. Getting together with Larry and Sandy, we thought up a party for the press at Midway as soon as there would be enough snow for skiing.

Sandy came down to ask Adina and me if we would help with the party. A friend had offered to cook up some soup. There would be cases of beer. It was a sunny day with a good snowfall. The press people, who had been brought up by Max in his jeep in several trips, came piling into the main room of the small shelter where some wooden tables and benches had been placed.

The kitchen had a good-sized wood range on which was simmering a big kettle of soup. Adina and I found eight heavy crockery soup bowls which had been used for the trail crew. We couldn't serve 30 to 40 people from these unless we could wash them in between. But, what to use for a dishpan? I spotted a big mixing bowl and filled it with hot water.

"That's all the hot water we got," the cook informed me, "unless you want to hike up the mountain to where there's water coming out of a pipe, or you could melt some snow."

"This'll do," I reassured him. After handing out the bowls of soup and madly washing the bowls in between, the water got greasier and greasier. We covered the washbowl with a dishrag so no one could see it. We stuck a bowl in, tried to wipe it clean, and then filled the bowl for the next guest. No one got ill and the write-ups were great.

71   We had been too busy with the soup to watch our kids. When it was time to collect the children we looked high and low for our four-year-olds, Sunni and Joanna. Eleanor and Rolf had been playing outside, coming in once in awhile to get warm. But where were Sunni and Jo? We finally looked in the back storage room where the cases of beer for the party had been stored. Some had been already opened to be handed out quickly. "We thought it was pop," said our girls in tears. Two sadder, dizzier little girls we had never seen.

Since we had to wait for the guests to be driven down to their cars below, Adina and I decided not to wait for a ride. Besides we felt fresh air would be the best thing for our two little gals. After putting on their skis, Adina and I skied down the road each holding a drooping child between our skis. Was it worth it? we wondered. We eagerly waited for what the press would write. The most poetic one I couldn't help but save for a future scrapbook:

*$150,000 Ski Area Underway In Colorado
Near Loveland Pass At 13,000 feet!*
Arapahoe Basin's superior features are six feet of powder snow, rolling slopes dropping down for miles, spruce forests, snow plumes streaming from the corniced ridges and swirling in gullies, and above all the glistening sunlight. . . . By next summer this new resort will have two chairlifts of modern design to whisk the skier from a parking area on U.S. Highway 6 to the summit of Norway Mountain at 12,000 feet. . . . Up there at the summit is being built the "Snow Plume Refuge," * a clubhouse with huge picture windows where guests can see the twilight sun tip the distant peaks, the massive cordillera of the Rockies, in an eerie golden light while purple shadows spread through the Valley of the Snake far below."

*We're still waiting for the "Snow Plume Refuge."

"So now we live in the Valley of the Snake," we laughed together, "and not in Montezuma Valley?"

7

"Vacations," Peaches and Silver

Sometimes we would get into projects completely removed from our ski life. One "vacation" concentrated on peaches, another on silver.

In early September, 1946, Adina and I had heard that fruit of all kinds could be had for almost nothing over near Grand Junction. After leaving the children with their grandmothers, we started off early one morning in Adina's old Studebaker. Our convertible wasn't big enough for all the fruit and produce we were planning to bring back. Neither of us had seen Glenwood Canyon or the Palisade country. The old car bounced noisily along. We were in high spirits even though the temperature at Glenwood Springs and from there west went well above 90°.

We had been told that the best peaches were to be found high on the mesa above the town of Palisade. Leaving the town, we climbed the dusty, narrow road up onto the flat mesa with orchards fanning out in orderly patterns. We soon came to a very neat farmhouse with a sign: "Peaches For Sale—Pick Your Own." We drove in and found the owner in the backyard.

"Sure," he said, "I got lots of peaches for you to pick."

"What do we pick them in?" we asked. "We didn't bring any baskets."

"Oh, that's no problem. Here, climb on the back of my truck and I'll drive you out to the orchard."

As we drove through rows of trees dust rose up around us and mingled with the rich smell of ripening peaches. When we got to a spot

73

he said would be good "pikkin'" he showed us how to balance the ladders against the tree branches. "What you do," he said, "is put on one of these." He handed us what looked like huge canvas aprons with one big pocket in the front and a drawstring at the bottom. Then he proceeded to show us how to fill the pocket. When filled, the string at the bottom could be released and the peaches would fall out into the basket below. We thanked him and started picking. These were Hales and the biggest, rosiest, juiciest peaches I'd ever seen or tasted.

"Isn't this great, Adina? This blue-blue sky, the green leaves, the rose-peach color of the fruit and that fantastic rose-peach colored cliff against the sky."

Our baskets filled fast. After moving the ladder around one time I must not have secured it too well. I felt like a kangaroo and probably looked like one too. Suddenly I felt my ladder start slipping. I grabbed a branch just as the ladder slid to the ground. I yelled to Adina. She quickly climbed down from her tree and put my ladder securely up. Then she burst out laughing. "You should have seen yourself dangling from that branch with that big canvas sack swinging from your neck and your feet kicking like mad." I couldn't help laughing too. I could picture it only too well.

"Let's call it quits." I felt we had more than enough peaches and my face was beginning to burn from the intense sun. "Why am I itching so?"

The farmer drove out to collect our baskets and charged us only $1.00 per basket. Enough peaches to can for a whole year. Then we drove down to the valley, stopping at fruit stands where we bought plums, melons, pears, tomatoes, beets, and beans all for a song.

"But this itching is terrible!" I looked at Adina and she was sunburned, her face shiny with all the juice from the peaches eaten while picking. She said, "We are covered with peach fuzz. Edna, I think we'd better rent a motel room and have a good shower. We've saved enough on the fruit and vegetables that we can afford a motel." "And a good supper," I added. "After all, this is supposed to be a sort of vacation day for us."

75   The next morning we started out early to get ahead of the hot sun.

Upon reaching Glenwood Springs we decided to drive into town for lunch. Coming out of the cafe we looked across the street to the movie house. *The Virginian* was playing. "With Joel McCrea," I exclaimed, "and I've always wanted to see it." In we went and were enthralled.

"A nice ending to our two-day vacation," I said to Adina as we approached the car. "Oh, No!" she cried out. Following her gaze I saw the flat tire. It was Sunday and the strollers, in their best church-going clothes, looked at us, two women in crumpled jeans and old shirts stained with peach juice. No help from them, we could see. "Well, here's where we learn to change a tire," Adina declared. "But we'd better get the spare out and see if that's O.K. We've still got over a hundred miles to go to get home."

"The garage up the street is open," one helpful man told us. We finally got the tire off, but in order to check the spare we had to unload all the produce on the sidewalk. We braced the melons with the baskets of peaches or they would have rolled down the hill and into the Colorado River. Adina rolled the tire up to the garage while I sat on the hood of the car and kept watch over our treasures. Then she came back and rolled the spare up the hill to the garage to have it checked. Finally, she returned and the garage man came with the spare. "I'd have put it on for you," he said, "but I'm alone up there."

"After you've done one you've done them all," Adina said. We put the tire back on, loaded in the spare, and piled in the fruit. The car was already redolent with mixed odors as home we went.

Our neighboring silver mining country had always fascinated us. During the war when we were stuck in "Dullsville," Washington, Max built a model, a relief map, of the area including Loveland Pass and Arapahoe Basin. It covered all the way past Independence Mountain, Keystone Mountain, and even showed Montezuma and Argentine Pass. It made us feel closer to Colorado to look at this model. We were intrigued by a number of mines he had marked for future reference.

The spring of 1952 was the spring we decided to explore the Peru

Creek country up near Argentine Pass. Our intention was to jeep up Chihuahua Gulch as far as the old mining road would let us. Then we climbed, carrying our skis, up the long snow field on 14,270-foot Grays Peak so that we could ski down.

Just above timberline we found a well-built two-story cabin. In front of the cabin was a small stream almost submerged by alpine primroses, marsh marigolds, and the garnet-colored king's crown.

That following week, Curly Mackie and Max checked out at the Court House on the status of the mines. They found the Rudolph Mine, where the cabin stood, had been patented in 1882. Most of the silver mines in the immediate area, they determined, were tax delinquent for over 50 years. We formed a small corporation for the 32 mines at Peru Creek. Then we bought a bulldozer and repaired the cabin. We hauled up a cookstove, bunks, mattresses, and food. The cabin could sleep nine, four downstairs and five upstairs.

Every Monday morning, Max, Curly, Rolf, Sunni, and our six-year-old nephew Teddy, would pile into the jeep. Nothing could dislodge them. They were all going "minding" as Teddy put it. I often joined them. It was too idyllic up there to be left behind. We broke even on the entire summer's work with the silver ore we shipped. It brought in just enough money from the smelter in Leadville to pay for the shipping charges. But what a summer!

8

"It's Easy, Edna, It's Downhill All the Way."

Snow came early that fall of 1946, and we were eager to ski Arapahoe, only five miles drive up the mountain.

We knew we would miss skiing at Climax and we'd miss our good friends, the Gorsuch family. But 35 miles one way each weekend, and only weekends, against being able to ski every day, was an exciting trade-off.

Max, with the help of Dillon mechanic Andy Rescola, had hauled up an old Ford motor engine for the rope tow.

Max tells about it:

> It overheated constantly at that altitude so we rigged up a big oil drum in place of the radiator for cooling. Earl was running the tow and using snow to cool the motor. He had started shoveling into the drum the more than four feet of snow that was within reach. About three weeks later, during which there had been a thaw, I returned from a trip back east.
>
> I had gone there to round up a few new stockholders for Arapahoe. To my astonishment there was about an acre of grass showing around that monster. I told Earl, "We may not have enough snow to ski on, but it looks like you found enough to keep the tow motor running."

We were all set. What a great winter this promised to be. Electricity had been brought into our old cabin at Ski Tip just before Christmas and we also had a phone. It was the only phone except the one down at Dimp's so it was in great use. Not having one up at Arapahoe yet meant that a lot of the immediate business was still being conducted in our kitchen. Sometimes I worried about not being able to pay the phone bill. However, it was all for a good cause, so we forgot about that item.

Over a cup of coffee with some friends in our kitchen, after a good day of skiing, someone said, "What we need is a ski club. There are lots of kids in this valley, at Breckenridge, Dillon, and Frisco, who don't know how to ski. Steamboat Springs has had a club for years and have a winter carnival every February. Also, Winter Park has kids coming up from Denver by train every weekend."

"Yes," I chimed in, "and even Climax has a ski club for youngsters and adults. Anyone from that mining town can join. And they have a racing program too. Jack and Zella Gorsuch work not only with their own children but they give hours of their time to the other kids too."

Max said, "I won't be surprised if one day we'll see some of those kids in the Olympics."

It was decided that I should phone all the local people we knew who might be interested. We met at the two-room schoolhouse in Dillon. A few parents and a number of youngsters came.

"What should we call our ski club?" someone asked. Since most of the skiing would be up at Arapahoe it was decided it would be the Arapahoe Basin Ski Club and our logo, of course we had to have a ski patch for our parkas, could be the ABC Ski Club. Someone wanted to know, "What does a ski club do?"

"This ski club's real purpose will be to help all the local youngsters to learn to ski. And there'll be those who'll want to learn to race. We'll have to find someone to teach ski racing too."

One parent spoke up, "There's the old Dillon jumpin' hill just north of town. We could use that as a beginners slope if everyone would be willing to help cut the brush that's grown up on the landing hill. Also, the kids could ski there after school since getting up to Arapahoe would take

80

too long for just the one or two hours they'd have before dark."

Everyone decided this was a "damn good suggestion." Anyone who could should show up and help the kids get the hill in shape.

News soon got around and on my next trip to the grocery store I was surrounded by old-timers. "We hear you're gonna rebuild the old Dillon slide."

"We might be doing some jumping," I answered, "but most of the skiing will be slalom."

"Why, that slide is famous," said one old-timer.

"Back in 1920 the world record was set on that jump by a young Norwegian, Anders Haugen. He jumped 214 feet, by gum. Ain't nobody seen such skiin' since." Being Norwegian myself, I was pretty pleased to hear of all these jumpers, Haugen, Hanson, Howelsen, Peter Prestrud, and Thor Groswold.

I met Peter Prestrud a few years later and heard him tell of the early days of jumping. "Why, we wouldn't think a thing of skiing over Ute Pass to Hot Sulphur Springs on Sunday to yump at a competition there. For our prize ve'd get yust a Hershey chocolate bar. All day ve vould be yumping and climbing up each time. Then ve'd yust ski all vay back to Dillon on our eight-foot yumping skis. In early fall dere vasn't enough snow at the bottom of the landing hill. So at the runout of the yump ve'd pile up all dis used hay—smell didn't bother us none." Listening to him tell me all this I couldn't help thinking that they were giants in those days.

With our four- and five-year-olds tagging along, Adina and I would climb up and down the landing hill cutting the brush. We would pack what snow there was this early in December so when more snow came we'd have a good base. As soon as school was out enthusiastic kids would join us. Some had the best of equipment such as the children of the Public Service Company employees and ranchers.

Their fathers would help since they had to drive in many miles anyway to pick up their children at school. "My offspring," one father said, looking up at the takeoff of the old jump above us, "can't wait to spring off of that."

It made me think, why not? Would it be possible to rebuild that jump? There were more important things just then.

Some of the eager children arrived with poor equipment. One youngster, I remember especially, had no ski poles, no hat or mittens, and an ill-fitting light jacket. It was cold on this north-facing slope. The sun dropped behind the hill even before school was out. His twisted seven-foot wooden skis had only toe straps. He had probably found them in an old barn near Dillon. Knowing the boy's mother, and knowing where I could find her, I parked my car in front of the Dillon Inn and went in. Being a bit "overstuffed" in the wrong places she not only draped over the bar stool but over the bar as well.

"Look here," I said as I approached her, "how about getting that boy of yours some decent ski equipment? He's too little for those long skis. He really needs a warm jacket, mittens, and something to keep his ears from freezing."

"Gee, Edna, I sure want to." She spun around on the bar stool to face me, being careful not to spill any of the bourbon in the glass she was holding. "Soon as I get a little money ahead, I'll get him what he needs. That damn ADC don't pay half enough to keep a soul alive."

It's hopeless, I thought as I left the Inn. Wonder what she meant by the ADC? Little did I realize then that in less than two years I would not only know, but would be typing the checks. The Aid to Dependent Children Program to which she referred certainly wasn't much help for her son.

We used long willow sticks for slalom poles and climbed, packed, and practiced along with the school kids. Standing in the starting gate with the late afternoon sun just touching the peaks to the east, I looked down the hill into the darkening valley with the lights of Dillon already turned on. My thoughts reached back to my first race, almost ten years before, in March 1938.

We had been married almost a year. Max had taken a year's leave of absence from Penn State to teach skiing in the Sierras. We lived at Cold Springs, California, where Max taught. This year I was to learn to ski.

82

I remember learning the snowplow and the stem turn, but the parallel turn or christie as it was then called, was difficult to learn. One day I found a book, which Max had brought along. It was by Charles Proctor, an already famous skier and instructor who was teaching over at Yosemite, not far away.

Glancing through the book, I found a chapter on parallel skiing, "The Pure Christie." I would quote from it here, but years later the book was "lifted" from the bookshelves at Ski Tip. Anyway, here was an idea for me to use to get the feel of how to do a christie turn. Stand on a small rug, preferably a rag rug, placed on a well-waxed wooden floor and then pretend one has just skied straight down a hill. Then suddenly push down the knees and push out the heels to one side, a sort of skate-hockey-stop.

I enthusiastically tried this on our cabin floor by first polishing a spot just the size of a small throw rug we had, then placing the rug over this spot. By running across the room and jumping on this rug, I could do just what the instructions said. Needless to say, I landed good and hard on my hip each time. To even up the black-and-blue bruises, I would try it from either side. I couldn't wait to try it on the snow. It worked beautifully, my hockey stop, until one day when the snow had softened from the warm sun and then frozen so we had a smooth but icy slope. Without steel edges it was like having my rug pulled out from under me. The icy snow was on a steep hill and not a flat floor, so that I kept sliding on my black-and-blue hips to the bottom of the hill.

"O.K.," Max said, "we'd better put steel edges on your skis. Then you'll have to learn to lean away from the hill on your turns."

By the time March came along I decided I'd like to try racing since there was to be a slalom race at this small Cold Springs area where Max was teaching. I looked down the course the morning of the race and assured myself, "It looks easy."

"Ready. Set. GO." I flew down through the first gate (there were five gates in all), made a turn, looked for the next gate, but there it was—above me. After finally reaching the finish, exhausted from climbing up to each missed gate someone asked me, "Didn't Max tell you to turn before the gate?"

"Max has been teaching seven days a week!" I answered. "I'm like the shoemaker's daughter. No time to sew me any shoes." I felt like crying. What a fool I must have looked. Needless to say I didn't finish very well, but I was hooked on racing—for life.

Max wouldn't let me quit. "I'm going to show you how to run some gates. It's late March and I've made enough money to get us through the summer, so I'll coach you this week. Next week we'll go up to Mt. Lassen where they are holding the California State Championships, and you can race in that."

"I'd love that." I was ecstatic as we practiced hard for a week. We

84

then left for northern California arriving at the Mt. Lassen area the night before the downhill.

Early next morning we were told to climb up past the jump, then follow through the woods on an old road and we'd come to an open slope. On up that open slope we would see the start. We climbed as fast as we could. It was difficult climbing up the road as there was a big hump in the center. Trucks and other vehicles had driven there until the snow had gotten too deep. Tracks of the wheels had melted making grooves on either side of the hump in the middle of the road. After reaching the open slope, we had to traverse back and forth as the start was quite a ways up the mountain. The women were to go first. There were only two gates, the start and the finish.

"The finish is at the end of the road," the starter informed us as he waved a flag hoping someone down there with the stopwatch, could see him. "Just stay on the road and you can't miss it." No one wore numbers then nor had any of us heard of wearing helmets.

I was terrified, knowing I'd have to schuss straight down to that narrow opening in the woods. Max, sensing my alarm, came over to me as I stood in line waiting my turn. "Don't worry, honey, you know you like to schuss. And, remember, *It's easy, Edna. It's downhill all the way.*"

Which really wasn't the case as I soon found out. I pushed off and headed straight for that opening in the trees which indicated the road. What I hadn't noticed while climbing was a sharp rise just before the road entered the woods. The speed I had wasn't enough to make this little uphill. I frantically herringboned up it, and then proceeded down the road.

The most terrifying part was still ahead of me. People were walking up to see the race. I shouted, *"Track!"* but they only laughed as they trudged uphill. Several even threw snowballs at me or at each other. I was busy trying to stay on the humped area in the middle of the road. I rounded a curve and saw all of a sudden a figure lying spread-eagle in front of me with a terrified expression on her face. She was the racer ahead of me. She had fallen and was too frozen with fear to get up. Yelling *"Track"* here couldn't help any, so I was forced to weave around the trees, then get back on the road. Finally I finished.

At the end of that day at the lodge I was thinking Max was wrong when he had said, "It's easy, Edna. It's downhill all the way."

"Did anyone," I asked, "make that uphill part of the downhill without having to herringbone up it?"

"Yup, you sure better bet. One guy made it," and someone laughed.

"Who?" I asked.

"Me. I raced that blasted downhill on my yumping skis. By yimminy, those yumping skis of mine can sure go fast." I looked up to see a six-foot-four blond Viking standing over by the fireplace.

"But," I was puzzled, "they mark your skis so you have to use the same skis for the downhill and the slalom. How will you ever race the slalom on jumping skis?"

"Oh, I don't do slalom, I yust yump."

"You're Norwegian, aren't you?" I asked delightedly. "So am I."

"You betcha. I'm Roy Mikkelson from Oslo, Norway, and I've yumped at Holmenkollen. You born there?"

"No," I answered regretfully, "but my parents were born there and my maiden name was Strand. Maybe that's why I love to ski so much."

The slalom was set the next morning on the golf course (!) with the start on top of a bunker. I believed it was set there to accommodate the spectators better.

"You still nervous?" the starter looked at me sympathetically. "Look here, take a swig of this brandy. Then you'll really relax and do fine." So I did, and a good hefty swig at that. I almost choked. After a moment I began to feel a bit dizzy, but breathed in great gulps of the cool air.

From the starting gate I looked down at the almost flat slope. This'll be a snap, I thought. The next thing I knew I had spun around the first gate. My ski pole had pulled off my mitten. I stood there hanging on to the slalom pole while I tried to reach down for my ski pole and mitten. Then I heard someone yell, "Hey, you're in a race. Get going."

"I am?" I looked up. "Well, I'd better ski down this thing. Gosh, I'm feeling dizzy." I did the splits and fell flat on my face right at the finish gate. Was Max ever *embarrassed*!

86

"Never again will you ever take a drink of anything the day of a race!" Max stated to me. He was really mad and disgusted with me.

"Oh, well," I laughed. "It was a lot of fun." Soon we headed down the mountain to the already green fertile valley of vineyards and back to Sonora.

Meanwhile—back in Colorado—

One day someone had a great idea. "Let's have a Winter Park kids' race day." I often wondered why it wasn't repeated. The next Saturday I had a phone call. "Bring all the kids over tomorrow, we're going to have a kids' race day."

There were only four from our area whose parents thought it would be O.K. One was our son, Rolf, age five. Adina and Earl thought Eleanor, their six-year-old might enjoy it. Earl and Max were both working at Arapahoe and Adina could not go so I would be the only driver. The other two racers were Jody Manly and Peter DeJuhasz, both high school students.

My nephew Peter was attending high school in Breckenridge that year. Neither had ever raced before.

Going to Winter Park meant driving over 12,000-foot Loveland Pass (still a dirt road), down to Georgetown, then up over 11,500-foot Berthoud Pass, and 12 miles down the other side to Winter Park. Snow tires were still not available so soon after the war, but we made it over Loveland Pass. However, there had been an avalanche on the east side of Berthoud Pass. All traffic was stopped. Finally the plows cleared an opening, and traffic started moving. We started to skid and spin. Out of the car jumped the two boys and pushed our little Ford until I got it moving. I didn't dare stop for them. How they ever were able to run, catch up, and jump in, I don't know, but they did. With a big sigh of relief we got to the top of the pass and headed down the other side to Winter Park.

We could see the gates all set up on the lower Hughes Trail. "You boys will have to find your own starting gate," I told them. "I'll have to stay with Eleanor and Rolf. This is their first race and they will have to start lower down."

"This is our first race, too," Jody yelled at me, but I was hard of hearing at that point. Little did we think we would make the front page of the Denver Post on Monday with the caption, "Pass the liniment, Pappy," which I thought should have read "Mommy" instead.

"If Mom didn't feel in the mood to cook breakfast," the news item read, "and Junior had a tough time getting out of the sack in time to make it to school, all hands are pardoned this Monday. Mom, Pop, and Junior had a big time at the Winter Park Ski Carnival Sunday." Under the heading, "SLAT JOCKEYS STRUT STUFF," was the following, "Twelve-year-old Buddy Werner of Steamboat Springs wowed the enthusiastic spectators with his daring slat riding." "Pug-nosed Werner," the article continued, "who stands about binding-high to a ski with his boots on, topped the Class C Juniors."

Then, further down the page, "Rolf Dercum, all of five-years-old, competed in this event with aid of his mother. Master Rolf also ran despite coaching from his second."

I was pretty unhappy with this comment. The moguls were so big that both Rolf and Eleanor could not see over them to the next gate. Somebody had to point out the next gate or the two of them would have been lost in the "Valley of the Moguls."

Farther down in the same news column, "John Bailey, chief of the Winter Park ski patrol, took part in the toboggan rescue demonstration." Sorry, John, we didn't stay for that. Anyway, we hadn't met you yet and didn't know that the following year you would become Dillon's new school teacher and principal, and the future Mayor of Dillon.

We made a hurried departure because we had to get over the two biggest moguls before reaching home—Berthoud and Loveland Passes.

The end of the season approached. Happily, someone decided that the annual May Day races would be at Arapahoe instead of Berthoud Pass Ski Area.

The first Sunday in May was a warm, sunny day. After working with the kids on the Dillon Hill, I thought I might be ready for this race. It was to be held on the Palivacini, or "Pali" as we called this ski slope. It was not in the Arapahoe Basin proper, but down the road, a bit west of the main ski area.

Everyone had parked on the highway at the bottom and climbed up to the start which was about halfway up the slope. There wasn't much breeze in this narrow-gully section where the slalom was set. The sun burned down on all 30 of us. Looking up to the large cornice overhanging the slope, I was glad we only had to climb halfway.

Since the lifts weren't built yet at Arapahoe, no one had been able to get over to this slope all year. Whoever put on the race (later I found out it was always the previous year's winners who placed first, second, and third) had chosen this slope so we could all park our cars at the finish.

I was a bit awed by the entrants. Among the famous skiers were Dick Durrance, Gordy Wren, Bob Kidder, Rudi Schnackenberg, George Engle, Florian Haemmerle, and a host of others. At the finish we all sat in the warm sun drinking snow-chilled beer and looking back up at the white ribbons our race tracks had made in the not-so-white spring snow.

It was only two days after the May Day race that Sandy Schauffler phoned from Denver. He sounded excited. "We've got someone who's really interested in investing in Arapahoe Basin—a couple from St. Louis. They have never seen any skiing and don't know a thing about it. But they've got $50,000 they could put in our ski area." Of course, uppermost on everyone's mind was the question, "Can we raise enough money this summer to build the two lifts and the shelter at the bottom?"

"Edna," continued Sandy, "we've got this idea, or call it an inspiration. Max could drive you to Midway today in the old jeep. I know the road up there is muddy as all heck now with the melting snow, but that jeep will go anywhere. You could ski across over from Midway to the North Glade and then cut across that over to the Pali. This way you'll be just about at the start of last Sunday's May Day Slalom. There are no flags left on the course, but the grooves left from the race should be pretty firm. We'll be at the bottom and watch you ski down."

"Sounds easy enough. I'll be glad to do it. Anything to sell stock. Also, a friend of ours, Jean Valens, is visiting us and I know she'll enjoy coming along. She's a good skier." (She later married Bill Bullard.) So it

89

was all arranged for us to get up to Midway about noon that very day.

After we strapped on our skis Max showed us the trail over to the North Glade. We set off while Max drove the jeep back down to the highway at the foot of the Pali. There he would meet Sandy and the St. Louis couple and await our beautiful ski exhibition of a fearless, speedy descent down the Pali.

It was starting to cloud up and we could hear thunder in the distance. "I believe," I told Jean, "we are going to have the first thunder and lightning storm of the season. We'd better get down to the highway before the lightning decides to strike all around us."

I led the way on sticky snow with Jean following about 30 feet behind. I noticed that the snow had pulled away from the rocks on the uphill side of the trail, leaving an airspace between.

All of a sudden, with no warning or sound, the trail under my skis dropped, and snow and rocks slid away out of sight. The snow had given way so quietly that I didn't realize it until I was flat on my stomach and sliding.

Fortunately I felt a rock scrape my arm. I grabbed it with my right hand. Holding on hard, I pressed my body to the slope. I yelled to Jean, who found me spread-eagle in this oh-so-steep gully. The rock to which I was clinging was below where my feet had been a few seconds before! I turned my head just enough to look below me and down this sickeningly steep couloir. I couldn't even see where the snow had gone, only the tops of the trees way below.

Jean took off her skis, crawled over the rocks above, then down by my right side to a small spruce. She secured herself by winding her legs in a scissors grip around the tree. Then she reached down and grabbed my arm with a solid grip. Her right arm was useless because of a recently dislocated shoulder so she had to pull me up with her left one.

"While I hang on to your arm," she quietly instructed me, "you try to wedge your lower ski onto that small projecting rock below you." I could not see the rock she referred to, but followed her specific directions.

By doing this, then pushing against the rock with my ski while she

90

91

pulled my arm, I was finally able to leverage myself to a safe position. At last I found myself standing next to Jean, but I began trembling like a quaking aspen leaf—so much so that I couldn't even talk. We just stood there for several minutes breathing deeply to steady ourselves. Then Jean put on her skis again.

"Come on! Where are you? Get moving." We could hear Sandy and Max yelling from the highway below. Also, the thunder kept getting louder. We realized they couldn't see us because we were hidden by the few trees below. We were very grateful because we didn't want "Mr. Rich" to be alarmed.

"I guess we'd better push on over to the Pali," Jean said. "We certainly can't go back where the trail used to be."

We reached the open slope of the North Glade and looked down to the highway where we were now visible to those waiting. "Come on! It's gonna storm!" they yelled at us. "Hurry up!"

But, there in front of us on the open snow of the glade was a six-inch-wide long deep crack arching across the snowfield. "Oh, Jean," I cried, "I'm afraid to cut across that."

"We'll try going above it," Jean decided. Most gingerly we traversed uphill and then quickly shot across and into the woods. Here the snow was wet and heavy, but it wasn't as steep nor so likely to slide. Clouds moved in front of the sun. Several flashes of lightning were followed by terrific echoing crashes of thunder. We reached the Pali at the point where the slalom start had been two days before. I had had fun racing down this course during the race. Now I was trembling so much, my legs feeling like wet noodles, that I could hardly ski.

At last we were at the bottom and there was Max and the jeep, but no one else. "Where are the others?" we both asked.

"The man's wife was frightened by the thunder and they left," Max explained. "But what on earth kept you two so long?"

"Oh! Just wait until we tell you." I was crying as I crept into the jeep and collapsed. It was just as well that the St. Louis couple and Sandy had gone.

There weren't any races the next year that I felt I could enter, being an old lady of 34.

However, Jackie Gorsuch Pyles had other ideas.

One day she drove over with her six-months-old baby, Scott. "There's a Southern Rocky Mountain Championship race down at Gunnison, Edna, and I'd love to enter. But I don't care to go down there all alone. If you want to come along we can both race. Friends of my parents say we could stay with them."

"It sounds great fun, Jackie, I'd love it." I was excited and knew Oma and Opa would be happy to take care of the children and feed Max too.

On checking our transportation we decided I should drive our Ford. This would leave Jackie free to tend to little Scott, whom she was still nursing, and therefore had to take him along.

We reached Gunnison in time to check out the race course a few miles north of town. Someone warned us to watch out for the last schuss on the downhill near the finish. "It has a sort of concave dip that can really throw you," we were told. It was a long downhill and scary enough without that, so I skied it more cautiously than I'd planned in the practice. Butterflies? I thought. Boy, I'm going to have more butterflies in my stomach on this one than for any other race I can remember.

The day of the race was bitter cold but clear. We parked the convertible near the warming shack. Scott was tucked into a cozy down sleeping bag and Jackie's friends said they would keep an eye on him. There was a rickety single chair lift up to the top where the start would be so we knew we wouldn't have to climb and be away from the baby too long.

There were no radios for communication to the bottom but there was a telephone hung on a tree near the starting gate. No non-stop trial runs were required in those days. I don't remember ever paying an entry fee.

There were no classifications of the racers. No questions were asked. You just entered and raced.

One of the young women who entered had just won the Roche Cup Downhill the month before at Aspen. She was telling us at the start, "This is the first year I've ever even skied. I love to go fast and if I stand up I'll win." Made me think back to my first downhill in 1938. But that one wasn't as steep, fast, or as long as this one. I kept that thought to myself.

Everyone was ready and the present Roche Cup winner was in the starting gate. "We'll wait till each one of you has finished before we start the next racer," the starter informed us.

"Thank God!" I was grateful as I could see myself halfway down, maybe crashed, and the next racer hurtling over a knoll and heading directly toward me. Too vivid an imagination isn't the best thing to have if you want to race, I kept telling myself.

She pushed off and soon disappeared. Jackie was next in line and already standing in the starting gate. We waited, and waited, and waited. The minutes went by and we began to wonder what had happened. Suddenly, the phone on the tree gave a ring. The starter grabbed it, listened, and kept saying, *My God! My God!"*

"What's going on?" Jackie had been standing in the starting gate long enough for the girl to have fallen, got up, and at last finished. "She must have gotten through the finish gate by now."

"She never went through the finish gate," the starter calmed down enough to inform us. "She started to fall near that dip at the finish and hit a kid at the side of trail. She broke his leg, flew through the air, and hit the timers' shack. Moved it two inches off its base and there were four men in the shack! They're waiting now to see how bad she's hurt. The ski patrol has stopped the race for awhile."

"Oh, golly!" Jackie moaned. "I've got a little baby in the back seat of Edna's car, and I've got to get down to take care of him." In spite of this problem we waited until the race resumed. We placed quite well even though we both checked for the lower schuss. We found Scott sound asleep. Twenty years later this rosy-cheeked Scott of the University of Denver ski team would win the International Intercollegiate Downhill in Innsbruck, Austria, in March 1968. As for the Roche Cup winner, we heard later that she had broken both legs and never raced again.

Every February Steamboat Springs held a winter carnival and we looked forward to it. The drive over was a long one on a winding dirt road that meandered around Green Mountain Dam to Kremmling and on U.S. 40 over Rabbit Ears Pass. The boys jumped besides racing in the slalom, so it was a two-day affair. We all wanted to see the night show on Steamboat's famous Howelsen Hill with ski jumping through fire-burning hoops. Also, that fellow from Utah who would ski down the hill with fireworks shooting from his head gear.

Sunday afternoon jumping on the big hill drew crowds from all over to see Alf Engen, Gordy Wren, Barney McLean, and Marvin Crawford, plus some visiting Norwegians.

Since all accommodations in town were taken, the ski club mothers arranged housing for us and the kids we brought along. The jury room of the Court House was our favorite. Here they put up double deck army bunks complete with bedding and blankets. The children loved having the whole place to themselves and would climb up into the judge's imposing chair and hold court. There would be a big town banquet on Sunday night with almost every entrant receiving prizes. Eleanor and Jo Ganong and Sunni and Rolf began to accept racing as a normal part of skiing. In fact, Sunni told me that she thought everybody in the world skied. It wasn't until she was almost ten when we visited Minnesota that she found out differently.

Having to wait around at the finish at Steamboat was a drag, so I thought I'd enter too. Again, I was accepted at my tottering old age. It was in '53 that Skeeter Werner asked me how old I was. When I told her 39, she exclaimed, "And still skiing?"

Someone else chimed in, "And let alone, trying to race!" This made me wonder, what am I doing here? But it was too much fun to drop it all.

The Rocky Mountain Division of the U.S. Ski Association decided to have racers classified into A, B, or C classes. One could enter a C race and if one did well, he could move up into the B class, and so on. Willy Schaeffler often brought his Denver University ski team up to Arapahoe. He never discouraged me from joining in the slalom training. I learned so

95

much from him that soon, after winning enough races, I had my B card and then my A. Going out of the starting gate faster and approaching the gates closer both helped tremendously. By holding a stop watch on us he made us strive even harder to peel off the seconds. Even though I have a won a number of medals, I have never gotten over the thrill of taking home a gold one.

In early March of 1953 the Divisional downhill and slalom races were at Winter Park. No helmets were required as yet. Even to this day I look with fear at that downhill course with the long schuss from "Norwegian Cut-Off" and the race down the entire Hughes! I remember my thigh muscles burning. That long last schuss still lay ahead of me. It was the most frightening and difficult downhill I have ever raced.

Buddy Werner, seeing my exhaustion at the end of the race, came over to me and said, "Look Edna, there are sections on that course where you can relax. That traverse before the last schuss isn't so steep, so relax. A good way is to feel real loose in the wrists, almost limp. Breathe deep, in through the nose and out through the mouth. Then, you'll be ready to attack that schuss." He was right and it worked and I got second in the combined. What a neat way to end the racing season, I thought.

Monday morning while I was cooking breakfast for the guests, the phone rang. One of the guests answered it and all of a sudden from the dining room came a great cheer. "Edna, come out here."

I wiped my hands on my apron and peered around the door. "What's going on?"

"You've been invited to race in the Nationals at Aspen this week," they shouted at me. "Congratulations, honey," Max was all smiles. "Since you got second in the Divisionals, you are automatically invited to participate in the Nationals."

"And you have to leave right away," the guest who'd answered the phone informed me. "Tomorrow they start practicing on the giant slalom."

"I'll go with you to keep you company driving over," our only ski-bum, Dorri, enthusiastically announced. She was our beautiful "Girl Friday," who made beds, waited tables, cleaned the johns, made the salads, and was learning to ski. "Hazel can get a girl from Dillon to help in the kitchen," said Max. "And, we'll all make our own beds," the guests chimed in.

We took off that afternoon with my trusty old seven-foot wooden skis. Helmets were still unheard of. Our good friends Toni and Ilse Woerndle from Garmisch had bought an old farm house for a ski lodge at the east end of Aspen. That would be where we would stay. We had a small room, no heat, an old iron double bed, but it was all very inexpensive. Everyone pitched in to help, which was confusing to Ilse, but made me feel right at home.

The first day we were told we could run the giant slalom for practice. It was icy, hard-packed and wide-open down Ruthie's Run. Andrea Mead Lawrence, Katy Rudolph, Sally Neidlinger, Janette Burr, and Skeeter Werner were there. I wondered what I was doing among these "youngsters," veterans of the '52 Olympics in Oslo. The icy giant slalom didn't help any. I could hear the scratch and bite of their skis long after they were out of sight as they tore down through the gates. I wanted to turn and go the other way but had no choice. Up at Arapahoe we had nothing but powder snow at our high altitude. I'd not heard skis scrape on ice since California.

The race was a nightmare for me and I came in next to last. At least I wasn't last and maybe the next day the downhill would be better.

Lovely Dorri had found friends, some former Ski Tip guests, who happily showed her the town. I would go to bed in the cold, cold room and try to sleep while running the downhill through my mind. When Dorri climbed in at 2 or 3 a.m. she said, "Gee, you're still awake! Don't think of that race. Go to sleep." So, I'd lie awake the rest of the night.

It was snowing heavily the next morning which delayed the start. I prayed it would snow forever and they'd have to cancel the whole thing. No such luck. The snow stopped before noon. Everyone had foot-packed the course and the racers were ready to start.

When I reached the second gate in my race it seemed to come up out of the snow and whack me around. The gates were heavy one-inch-square wooden poles. To me they felt and looked like two-by-fours. I got up and somehow in my glazy-eyed nightmare state found the finish at the bottom of Spar Gulch.

Willy Schaeffler, racing too, came up to me the morning of the slalom. "Just think you're back practicing slalom at Arapahoe, Etna," he said, with his German accent. "It's an easy slalom." And it was easy, short and familiar. I ended up in the first 10 in the combined, and got a sixth in my first slalom run. Did I ever sleep well that night.

Meanwhile, back at the ranch, the cook Hazel had threatened to quit. But the young girl Max had located from Dillon, who was eager to make a little extra money, was a gem. Hazel was appeased. She announced to me the morning we returned home from Aspen, "Why, that girl saved me from having to wash the extra forks for the dessert. When we had pie she told all the guests, as she was removing their dinner plates, 'Hold your forks, folks, hold your forks.'" I laughed while picturing our sophisticated Chicago guests holding their forks in the air and wondering, "What now?"

9

Court House Daze

In the fall of '48 the snow came early, loads of it, in October. Max and Earl, who'd both been working for Dimp, came down Grizzly Gulch from road building at the Hunkidori Mine. Next day we all headed up to Arapahoe. Having worked the year before, Earl at the Midway lift, and Max on the top of Norway Mountain, they expected they'd be running the lifts again.

But, lo and behold, there were no jobs! The Arapahoe Basin Corporation had hired an entire new crew from Georgetown. It was a shock to all of us.

"Come on, let's go skiing," Max said to me. "If I'm out of a job, I'll just ski."

I felt depressed and worried, but followed him up in the single chairlift which he and Earl had helped to build two summers before. It was a beautiful day with perfect powder snow. "Maybe it'll all work out, I hoped. Soon we found ourselves laughing and forgetting everything but the aliveness of floating down—down—through that fantastic snow.

We had stopped to rest in the bowl of the Davis Trail when a tall blond man skied up to us. We had watched him earlier and I had remarked to Max that this fellow must be a racer. He skied the steepest trails so easily and yet faster than anyone I'd ever seen.

"Let me introduce myself. I am Willy Schaeffler." He took off his glove and we all shook hands. "I've just been hired to run the ski school here. I watched you skiing, Max, and wondered if you would like to teach for me. I heard from someone that you have passed the ski instructor's certification."

Willy explained, that since he had already accepted the position as ski coach of the Denver University ski team, he really needed someone capable of teaching for him up here at Arapahoe. "And," he promised, "you'll be my head instructor. If possible, in the future, maybe a co-director."

"What luck, Max," I said. "After all, you really weren't cut out for sitting in that wind and snow-blasted shack on top of Norway Mountain all winter." Our early fall skiing was off to a good start.

Everyone was talking about the upcoming elections. I had voted back in Pennsylvania in 1936 and 1940. I decided I'd better register so I could vote in Colorado and in Summit County. Someone at the Court House asked me what I was, a Democrat or a Republican?

I was puzzled and answered, "I don't know what I should be. Up here in the mountains we read the *Summit County Journal,* but the news is all local news. I don't know what's going on out there in the outside world."

Realizing I wasn't a good citizen, I tagged along one day with Oma and Opa over to Breckenridge where they registered as Republicans. I felt I would like to be Independent so put down no affiliation. Opa said, "You should be something, Edna. Otherwise you'll be a mugwump."

"What on earth is a mugwump?" I asked.

"It's a bird," Opa laughingly informed me, "who sits on the political fence with his mug on the one side and his wump or tail on the other."

"Even so," I thought, "I'll wait awhile and see which side of the fence to choose."

I was aware that Opa had agreed to run for the office of Country Clerk and Recorder. I had promised him I would be his deputy until the next spring, if he won, when he was sure he could find someone to take my place. With the two children at home, and Rolf just starting first grade we felt that three months would be all I should work. Since I could type, it would be a help as the office had no photostat or copy system. We really felt Opa needed the job. He had spent everything on the house and helping us with building our basement, the well, and the squared-timber wing at Ski Tip.

Winning the election became important to the whole family. It looked as if we'd all be scratching for some kind of income. None of us realized that both Oma and Opa, being over 65, could have drawn old-age pensions, and Opa social security. Both payments were well over what he'd make as county clerk. This was one case of ignorance not being bliss.

Opa and I would get into his little Ford and go campaigning "down the Blue" (river), up to Breckenridge, and over to the mining towns of Montezuma and Kokomo.

Sometimes we took turns to go electioneering. One day I drove up to the door of a low log ranch house. The door stood open and a voice called out, "Come on in. Don't mind the chickens. Shoo 'em aside and they'll get outta your way."

The friendly stout woman pulled out a chair at a round oak table and invited me to sit down. Most of the table was heaped with papers and dishes except for one side where she was stirring batter in a big crockery mixing bowl.

"I'm bakin' up a batcha cookies," she said. "Here have some, fresh outta my oven." Happily I took a couple of the delicious crisp cookies, then two more.

While I was munching on the cookies she kept up a stream of talk. The ash bin of the big cookstove was full to the brim. It was pulled out to leave more room under the firebox for ashes to fall directly onto the dirt floor beneath.

In the middle of the room was a barber stool with a red plush cover. It had a foot pedal so it could be pumped up. Evidently this enabled a person to be closer to the one light bulb hanging overhead from a long cord.

"That's my brother's chair," I was told. "He likes to sit there and read the newspaper."

101

As I explained my election campaign the chickens scurried in and out of the room pecking crumbs. The woman broke eggs into the batter. One egg rolled off the table onto the dirt floor. Without stopping her chatter she tore off a piece of the egg carton, scooped up the egg from the floor, and dropped it into the batter.

"Here, have another cookie," she said. I declined, thanked her, saying I must get on my way.

"You'll sure have my vote," she screamed after me. "Come by any time. I'll put on the coffee pot and we'll have some more cookies."

At the end of a long Sunday of campaigning Opa and I were greeted by a sun-bronzed rancher.

"Running for Country Clerk and you want my vote, Mr. Dercum? Guess you know you're not very well known around here." Then his eyes crinkled as he smiled. "But, on the other hand, maybe your opponent is too well known."

I guess that is how we won and by a comfortable margin.

Opa and I were to be sworn in on one of those January days when you'd swear spring had come. A warm chinook breeze blew down over Breckenridge from the Ten Mile Peaks. As I walked up the steps of the Court House I looked up to Peak Ten with its snowfields glistening in the morning sun.

I'll miss not skiing except on Sundays, I thought to myself. This is necessary if we are to survive, but it won't be forever. As we opened the door to the hall, the stifling overheated air, redolent of stale oily floor wax, assailed us.

This is it. Now we've really done it. I wondered to myself, can we handle it? We were greeted by the three commissioners, two of them rancher friends. We felt better.

The retiring County Clerk, Elva Jane, was a handsome young woman. She had chosen not to run again as she had recently married and wanted more time in her new home. However, she said she'd be happy to stay on for a week to help us. She was a good Republican she told Opa, but she looked questioningly at me. Still a mugwump? I thought to myself.

Politics and government buildings had never interested me. But now

102

that I was a government employee, I was curious. Across the big square hall from our office was the County Treasurer's office. Next to this was the County Assessor, then the County Attorney. Across the way was the Sheriff's office, then the Commissioners' and then back to ours, the Country Clerk and Recorder.

In the middle of the hall toward the back was a wide oak stairway. At the halfway landing the stairs separated, one side going only to the District Court and the Judge's chambers. The other side approached the Welfare Office, the County Court, and beyond this was the District Court Clerk. Underneath the first floor stairway and at the back was the stairs which descended to the one-cell jail, the driver examiner's, the janitor's quarters and the rest rooms. I noticed that the jail was right under the commissioners' room and extended partway under our office.

During the first afternoon, while we were trying to learn the "ropes" of the office, we were serenaded by lovely clarinet music. "Where's the music coming from?" I asked Elva Jane.

"Oh, that's the prisoner down in the jail. When you go down to the rest room you'll notice the jail door is open. Makes it more convenient for him so he can go down to the Gold Pan Bar for his meals and any beer he wants to bring back. The sheriff will lock the door at night so he can't escape. We don't often get any prisoners here, especially music-talented ones. You might as well enjoy it while you can."

It was the most confusing day of my life. Motor vehicle license sales and renewals came due at noon, one hour after we'd been sworn in. The bonding process was very simple. We simply signed the official ornate documents. "You are bonded now," we were told.

I thought, bonded? Isn't that something that went out with the Civil War and slavery?

Driver's licenses were due that day also. It seemed everyone in the entire county was lined up in front of the long front counter. Elva Jane, untiringly, tried to show me how to make out the different licenses, the fees, and the ownership taxes.

There were solid brass spitoons placed everywhere the janitor thought necessary. One was in front of the counter near the door, and

104

another one behind our long slanted counter. I was always tempted to see if I could hit the mark from my high stool, but I could never get up the courage, or the saliva.

A day or so later I'd gotten the hang of making out the licenses, so was left on my own at the front desk. A young man had come in with his little boy. It was very quiet except for Opa's "peck, peck" on the typewriter. I struggled to make sure I made no mistakes on the license. Suddenly I heard a sound. Looking up at the young man, whose face was becoming redder and redder, I realized his little boy had hit the mark. When you gotta go, you gotta go. There never was a more conveniently placed "potty" and brass yet.

Off to the side of our office was a big walk-in safe. All the walls were lined with books, not small books, but huge ones. They were so tall and thick and heavy it was all I could do to lift them. I looked at the black titles on the grey canvas covers, Grantor, Grantee, Deeds of Trust, Leases, and so on. There were also heavy books handsomely bound in red leather with all the titles in gold; Location Certificates, Mining Deeds, Affidavits of Labor, and others. I pulled one out at random and opened it to the date of 1885.

Then I noticed a couple of dog-eared books on the floor under some shelves and pulled one out. "Commissioners Proceedings," was written in fine Spencerian script on the front cover. The date was of the turn of the century, 1900-1905. Glancing through I read where the commissioners were arguing the feasibility of purchasing a team of work horses for road building. While turning the pages I came upon, "The Madam of the Blue House came in and paid her monthly fine." I took the book out to Elva Jane. "It will be great fun reading through all of this," I told her.

She laughed. "If you'll find the time, Edna. The biggest part of your job here is to type and proofread all the deeds that come in, plus the cross-indexing. You'll burn the midnight oil proofreading because you sure as hell can't do it when you're constantly interrupted making out vehicle licenses, driver's applications, game and fish licenses, or just visiting with anyone who wants to drop in to gossip. Remember you don't turn off anyone. They're your next vote."

I had seen the sign hanging in front of our desk counter for all to read:

IF YOU ENJOY WORK, YOU'LL SURE HAVE
A HELL OF A GOOD TIME IN HERE

Guess she's right, I thought with sinking heart. I hadn't planned on working nights too. Sunday would be my only full day to be with the children and my only time to ski with them. Oh, well, it's just till May when Opa will have found a deputy to take my place, I comforted myself.

The phone rang, interrupting my thoughts. I told Elva Jane I would answer it.

"Hi there," a cheerful voice answered. "Is this the new County Clerk? This is Carl Breeze and I'm President of the Bank of Kremmling. I'll have to come in and introduce myself."

I explained that I was only the deputy. He said, "Well, you can help me. I need a lien search on a chattel mortgage."

He might as well have asked me in Greek. "What's a chattel mortgage? This is only my third day here. Wait, I'll put Elva Jane on the line." I was desperate. What a dummy he must think me. Chattel? Did that have something to do with cattle?

After Elva Jane hung up, she laughed. "He's coming in tomorrow. Said he'd never met anyone who didn't know what a chattel mortgage is."

I defended myself. "We've never, the Dercum family, us, my Mom, none of us have ever had anything to do with mortgages. We've always saved up until we had the money to buy what we needed."

"You'll learn a lot about mortgages and borrowing and lien searches in here. You'll watch as the County Treasurer, who is the Public Trustee, sells a bankrupted man's property on the front steps of the Court House. I assure you, you'll learn a lot of other things too, but I'll just not list them now." Elva Jane's assurance made me think maybe I didn't want to be assured.

One day, a young, dark-complexioned fellow came in to apply for a driver's license. After making out the application, I directed him to the **106** driver examiner's office in the basement where he would be given the full test. After the exam the applicant would return to our office for his temporary license, provided he'd passed.

This time, as I was making out the young man's temporary license, I noticed the examiner had accompanied him and stood to one side and waited until the fellow had left. I could sense the examiner wanted to talk so I looked up.

"Them Mexicans sure am dumb," he informed me.

"Why?" I asked, surprised. "He passed the exam, didn't he?"

"Well, ya," he explained. "But, would you believe it? He didn't know what a presbyterian was!"

"A Presbyterian?" I was astounded and bewildered. "But, why on earth? What has a Presbyterian to do with a driver's exam? What do you mean, a Pres—Presbyterian, what, what?" I stuttered.

I could see his opinion of my intelligence go way down. "A presbyterian," he informed me in a condescending voice, "you know, is them people what walks across the street."

The next week went by and I dreaded Elva Jane's leaving. She and I both worried about Opa's "peck, peck" with two fingers at the typewriter. She confided in me, "You'd better let him take the front desk and you do the typing. He'll get so far behind with those deeds that he'll never catch up."

"But he hates the front desk," I told her. "I can see he's getting frustrated and worried while all these deeds and papers are piling up." Driving home that evening, he voiced his frustration. "I should never have run for this office. It's a stinking job. Do you know, Edna, that we don't get any vacation? I'll never get out to see our daughter in Washington and the grandchildren there. And I'll probably die in that office. It's the only job I can see ahead of me. There's no work for an architect up here and probably never will be."

"Oh, Father," I tried to sound assuring, "don't worry. Things will ease off and come spring I should get the hang of all this. I'm sure I could handle the office for a couple of weeks by myself." It didn't sound like much, I felt sure, to a man who had been as independent and successful as he had been.

The following Monday came and with it a driving blizzard. We had a 20-mile drive from home to Breckenridge. This day the wind and snow blew so hard across the gold dredging fields that we had to stop often and scrape the freezing snow off the windshield of the old Ford. It was to be our first day alone in the office. It seemed so bleak not to have Elva Jane there to greet us.

There was a ski club meeting that evening at the high school so I told Opa to go home at five. I would finish up the accounting of receipts and cash, which was always done after locking the door. Also, I thought I could get at the typing and maybe make a dent in the pile of deeds.

"I can get a ride home with Adina and Earl, who'll be at the meeting. Drive carefully in this storm. Don't forget to pick up the groceries that Oma wants from Dillon."

The ski club meeting lasted longer than I thought. The next morning, my day to drive, I pulled up in front of Oma and Opa's house. No one came out. I was in a hurry, being a bit later than usual. Having to get the kids ready for school, packing their lunches and mine and Max's, and piling the kids into the car, had taken longer than usual. I finally rushed into the house and was met by Oma.

"Shh," she shushed me. "Father sort of collapsed last night. Don't know what's wrong. He complains of feeling sick to his stomach so I made him stay in bed today. Oh, Edna," she was close to tears. "I'm afraid this job is too much for him. He's so worried he can't handle it, since he can't type, you know. But, we need the money. It's not much but it will buy the groceries and pay the bills."

"Things will work out, I'm sure of it." I tried to comfort her. Running back to the car in a hurry to get the kids to school and myself to work, I knew I wasn't sure of it or anything much else.

Opa remained at home and seemed to improve the next few days. "I'll be able to be on deck next Monday," he told me on Friday evening. I told him that the week had been a quiet one. Elva Jane had dropped in often to help.

On Saturday morning I drove Sunni and Rolf down to Oma's since

108

I'd have to work until noon and Max would be up at the Basin teaching skiing. After balancing the accounts and catching up with the mail, I knew it would be mid afternoon before I'd get home.

I opened the office door hurriedly because I could hear the phone ringing. It kept on ringing. O.K., O.K., I'm coming. Someone for another lien search, I thought.

But it was Max. "Edna, I'm calling from Mother's." I knew before he told me. "Father just died."

"Oh, God! Oh poor Opa." I started to cry.

Elva Jane, the treasurer and the sheriff were standing in the doorway in shocked silence. After a moment, Elva Jane came into the office. "We're closing the office, Edna. You go right home."

The Court House was closed through Tuesday, the day of the funeral, in honor of Father. We never knew we had so many friends. People came to the house with hot casseroles and other food. They would stay with mother telling her what a fine man they thought Father. It helped so much. This was a custom we had not known existed and certainly was not practiced back east. They even brought alcoholic beverages, and made us sit down and have a nip with them. All their friendship and kindness gave us the sustenance we needed.

Wednesday morning I slowly walked up the front steps of the Court House. It had been just two weeks ago that Father and I had both entered together. Elva Jane was waiting for me to open the door.

"What do I do now?" I felt too dejected to think about it. "I'm neither fish nor fowl. Not even a deputy, only acting until Opa's position would be filled by appointment by the County Commissioners.

"Well," Elva Jane told me in a matter-of-fact way, "next Monday is the Commissioners' meeting and they will have to appoint a new county clerk. Since there are three commissioners, two of them Democrats, no doubt a Democrat will be appointed. Your father-in-law won as a Republican, but the commissioners don't have to take that into consideration, you know."

I didn't feel much of anything except sorry for Father and all the work he'd put into running for this office. "By the way," I told Elva Jane,

Fall   Rolf Dercum

The green of summer
  sinks back into the earth
Leaving the world
  to rusty autumn
Skies darken
Animals scurry about storing food

Then suddenly —
  all is quiet before
  the first storm of winter

"Opa's insurance, even after he'd borrowed on it, will leave Oma with a comfortable $9,000. Somehow, Max and I will make out. Maybe I could try teaching skiing too."

Cleaning out Opa's drawer, I found a small pen and ink drawing. It was of himself, seated on a high stool at a desk, peering under an eyeshade at a big book spread out in front. Somehow it looked like a sketch out of a Charles Dickens book. I remembered his lovely architect's office in Cleveland, having lunch with him in the elegant private Athletic Club, and meeting his colleagues. I remembered his last words to me, "It's a stinking job." He'd asked his fellow citizens to vote for him. I knew he would never have quit or given up.

The day of the Commissioner's meeting came. Earl Rice, a Democrat and a quiet, intelligent man came early. I remember Opa had said to me, "I admire this man, this rancher with his good common sense." He was accompanied by his wife, Josephine, an attractive, self-possessed woman, not given to a lot of talk. I had gotten to know her, and many other rancher's wives, in the Home Demonstration Club. I had learned that when she did say something, which was seldom, it was worth listening to.

Earl strode over to my desk and stated, "You ran on that ticket as much as your father-in-law did. The people voted for you too. You'll be the next County Clerk, Edna."

I couldn't keep back the tears and put my head down on the desk. Did I really want the office? But, now, I too had a duty to the voters. I raised my head and said, "Thank you, Earl."

"I'm spending the day here," Josephine announced, as she seated herself on a chair in front of my desk. "You'll need all the support you can get today."

I soon learned what she meant. Several people streamed into the Commissioners' room, among them the Chairman of the Democratic party, the County Attorney, and several other staunch Democrats. The day wore on and I could hear raised voices, some quite angry. "Here's our chance to get a Democrat in that office." Finally, late in the afternoon, I turned to Josephine, who was sitting relaxed near a window watching the people come and go. "How can Earl hold out against all that?" I asked.

110

Quietly and with a smile she looked at me. "He gave you his word, didn't he?" I heard the front door slam, hard enough to almost shake the solid brick building. "There go the Attorney and the others. Now, you are our new County Clerk, Edna." And all I wanted to be was a ski racer!

The next morning Elva Jane and I tried to get down to business but people kept coming in. Helen Rich, the writer, came down from the Welfare Office, where she and Susan Badger held sway.

Helen, I knew was a Democrat, but her boss was a Republican. Susan Badger was a big woman, a dignified one from the state of Maine as she often reminded us. We all called her *Miss* Badger. No one called Helen anything but Helen. I noticed on Helen's Game and Fish license that the color of hair was listed as "grizzled," at her insistance.

Miss Badger would always arrive later than the rest of us with her little black cocker spaniel pulling on the tightly-held leash. It made me think of a stately steamer being towed into harbor by a small tug. But Miss Badger had a wonderful sense of humor. While awaiting the arrival of the commissioners she would tell us some salty stories. She had us laughing so hard that when the three commissioners came in the door they looked at us askance. Miss Badger would straighten up with the most dignified bearing and as the commissioners filed past her, she would announce in a loud voice, "These three, these immortal three."

Helen Rich had had one novel published and was hard at work on another. She had grown up in Sauk Center, Minnesota, a childhood playmate of Sinclair Lewis, "or Red Lewis we all called him. By the way, I think my new book will be a success. Just heard that Agnes Miner built a bonfire and burned my latest novel down on Main Street right in front of her house. Had too much sex in it for old Agnes, the so and so WCTUer. And, Edna, I'll be bugging you for items for this next book. You'll have to give with the scuttle-butt. With me, it's in one ear and out my typewriter."

"By the way, did you know that this county is 90% Democrat?" she informed me. "Now you know who put you and your father-in-law in office."

"But," I retorted, "I ran on the Mugwump ticket."

She laughed, "Come on over after work for a drink. You look like you need one. Anyway, I want you to meet Belle Turnbull, another writer who lives in the cabin with me. She's a graduate of Vassar, like your mom-in-law, class of '04. We'll celebrate your dubious victory with a boiler-maker."

That evening I relaxed for the first time in weeks, enjoying the boiler-maker. An open fire was burning in their beautiful old Franklin stove with its cranberry-colored tiles. Their cabin was old too, but well-built. There was a lovely glow to the room with the Persian rugs on the random-width, wood-pegged floors.

"I understand you're a Vassarite, Miss Turnbull?"

"Oh, Edna, don't call me Miss Turnbull. I'm Belle to my friends. To answer your question, or accusation, all I can say is that Vassar never prepared me for life in Breckenridge." She laughed, looking like a delicate Dresden figurine with her rosy cheeks, sparkling blue eyes, and her beautiful white-white hair.

Belle was just the opposite of Helen who chopped and stacked the firewood for their stoves. Belle had come to Summit County several years before to recover from tuberculosis, or "consumption" as they called it in those days. Belle insisted she felt stifled below timberline and she loved this high mountain country and its people. She worked hard at her writing and was just finishing her third book, an earthy mixture of poetry and prose, *The Ten Mile Range*.

Soon we had copies of their books. My favorite inscription to us was by Helen in her book, *The Willow-Bender*. "To Max and Edna, who love the mountains, and their people too."

Looking around for a deputy wasn't easy. There weren't that many who wanted to work five-and-a-half days a week for $150.00 a month. However, I was lucky to find Cleta, a very attractive and intelligent woman. Her husband's business required him to be gone a great deal, and with her children grown and gone from home, she welcomed the diversion. She also knew all about withholding statements, Social Security forms, and others. As I was soon pleased to find out, officious people didn't bother her.

One day I had a phone call from Denver. Cleta, my deputy, had answered, but she said to me, "It's person to person for '*that* County Clerk up there.'"

I took the phone and a man's voice gave his name and shouted in my ear, "You the County Clerk?" Upon my acquiescing, he continued, "This is the Department of Revenue. Do you know you could be sued on your bond for what you've done?"

"Done?" I stammered. "What-w-w-what have I done?"

"You're short 75 cents on the car title fees you sent in. Of that fee of $1.00 you collect, you're supposed to keep 25 cents for your office and send in the balance to us. Of the 23 car titles you sent in this month you made a mistake in sending 25 cents on one of them and not 75 cents. I'm warning you to send that 75 cents in right away." I thought after he'd slammed down the receiver, it should be 50 cents. He's already received 25 cents of the 75. Big deal.

"What was that all about?" Cleta asked. After I explained it all to her, she said, "One lousy mistake of 75 cents. You get right back on that phone and call person-to-person to that guy. I'll stand right here by you. You just repeat right after me what I tell you."

Contacting him on the phone, I asked, "Is this Mr. Nitbitcher?" (I don't dare use his real name.) "Yes, go ahead, whadayawant?" I could hear him snarling out the words.

"This is the Summit County Clerk you just called." Cleta reached over and grabbed the phone. "And you can go to Hell!" She slammed down the phone.

That was the last we ever head of Mr. N. or the Department of Revenue. Needless to say, I was very careful after that to send every correct penny.

After making out all those car titles and filing the liens, I noticed almost 100 per cent were mortgaged. Our old Ford was burning up at least $30.00 a month in oil. My $8.00 per day pay was before withholding tax. Maybe, we should get a new car and live on credit like everybody else.

After discussing it with Max, down to Idaho Springs I drove one Saturday afternoon. I traded in the old Ford, and returned home with a new Plymouth station wagon. It was the first all metal station wagon that Plymouth had put on the market. I was scared to drive it over Loveland Pass on the way home since the road was being rebuilt and all torn up. I didn't want the new car to get the least bit dusty so drove over paved Berthoud Pass. I proudly arrived at the back door. Max was still using the army jeep he'd bought for $25.00.

The next morning, as I parked it in front of the Court House, everyone came out to admire it. While standing around and discussing its virtues, the sheriff came tearing out of the Court House.

"Quick, Edna, get back in your car. We have an emergency and I'm requisitioning you and your car. I'll tell you about it on the way out."

Grabbing my purse and coat, I yelled to Cleta, "Carry on, old girl. Don't know what it's all about."

We drove like mad to Frisco while the sheriff filled me in. "The hearse, I mean the ambulance, is down in Colorado Springs in the garage. Maybe you didn't know but the local undertaker is the County ambulance driver and his hearse is the ambulance. This is an emergency. A lady in Frisco has a ruptured hernia and the local nurse is with her. We'll have to rush her in to Colorado General Hospital right away."

Now, I thought, I understand that sign one sees by the highway as one drives into Dillon:

PLEASE SLOW DOWN!
DILLON IS A ONE-HEARSE TOWN!

"There's no other station wagon in the County," the sheriff continued. "We'll put an army cot catty-corner in here. The nurse can sit on a camp stool in the back in case she has to use the needle if the lady comes to."

Arriving in Frisco, two men loaded the patient, and the nurse climbed in. "You'll have two more passengers," the sheriff told me, "but they'll sit up front with you."

I looked to see who these passengers were. Here came a man with no

114

legs, pushing himself ahead with his hands. His body was on a round disk which had small wheels. The sheriff hoisted him onto the seat next to me. Then another man got in so we were three across on the front seat.

"This here is the woman's husband," the third man announced. "I'm the undertaker. I'm going along in case you need any help."

"Well, if you're going to be of any help," the nurse said, "you can hold this hypodermic needle for me. It's filled with morphine, but it's all wrapped in cotton batten. Handle it carefully. I might need it if she begins to come to." The undertaker took the needle, holding it in both hands.

Over Loveland Pass we headed, soon going 80 miles an hour. I thought to myself, I was the one who once had said, you'll never catch me driving this pass.

Loveland Pass was a winding, bumpy dirt road. At one point we were halted by the road crew just as they were pulling a big tree across the road. The undertaker jumped out, shouted to the men. Soon they had cleared a way through for us. "The sheriff radioed ahead," the undertaker informed me. "There will be a state patrolman at Idaho Springs. He'll drive ahead of us and give us clearance."

We reached Idaho Springs and beyond. No patrolman showed. Over Floyd Hill, and on over Mount Vernon road, all two lane roads, we tore. We arrived at the hospital on the east side of Denver and into the ambulance entrance in one-and-a-half hours from Frisco.

The nurse asked the undertaker for the needle. "Why it's empty!" she exclaimed.

The undertaker looked at her sheepishly. "Guess I got so nervous at the speed we was travelin' I musta kept plungin' it into that wad of cotton."

"Good thing she didn't need it," the nurse mumbled angrily.

As the nurses were wheeling the woman into the hospital, I looked at the white car with lights flashing which pulled up behind me.

"Lady, I tried to catch you all the way from Idaho Springs, but boy, were you traveling!" He added, "Your shiny new car ain't so shiny no more. Saw it in Idaho Springs yesterday just 'fore you bought it."

With so many days of working indoors, I treasured Sundays. When it wasn't ski season we would try to work outdoors on Sundays, peeling the logs for the new addition, or cutting winter firewood.

One golden fall day we decided to explore above the old town of Tiger and up into the area known as The Swan. Max's old army jeep would go anywhere. We drove up a dusty logging road until we came to where it ended. Oma, the children, and I found a faint trail winding up through the tawny above-timberline grass. While Max explored an old mine dump, we climbed up and around a low hill. The wind was strong making the dry grasses wave with a sighing sound, "Winter is coming."

All of a sudden, around a curve of the hill, we saw an old log cabin. What a cold, windy place to build a cabin, I thought. The door stood open and we entered right into a kitchen. The wood stove was covered with newspapers. They were recent, not old papers of years ago, but only a year old.

"What a horrible smell!" I exclaimed. "It seems to come from this room off the kitchen." I tried to push open the door but could only get it to open a couple of inches. The odor was overpowering. Rolf said, "Maybe a bear got in there and couldn't get out and died."

I decided we'd better get out. "This cabin is in really good condition," I said. "I'd like to explore it more if it weren't for that awful smell." Shepherding the youngsters, Oma and I soon joined Max. He was more interested in the ore samples he was finding.

The next morning, back at work at the Court House, I mentioned our day's adventure and the old cabin. The sheriff had come in to check on a driver's license and overheard me. "Where is this cabin, Edna?" he asked. I tried to tell him just where it was.

It was about noon of the next day when the sheriff came back into the office. "I've got a jeep and driver out here and I want you to come with us. Show me where that cabin is that you found last Sunday, Edna." It being a beautiful fall day, I had no objections.

About two hours later we came to the spot where we had parked our jeep, and started climbing. The wind was still whistling through the

The County Court House dominated four years of my life, and Breckenridge.

Spring of 1946 we decide to tear down the old log outbuildings and the back wing.

After cutting the logs we load them with Max's cat and A-frame.

With my 4-year-old supervisor I spruce up our old cabin with its new log wing.

117

The old cabin sprouts wings in all directions—on the south a dining room and living room take shape.

Curly helps Max build the north wing with 4 bedrooms.

On the north wing I painted my "upside-down" balcony.

118

grasses as we wound our way up and around the hill.

There was the cabin, just as I had seen it two days before.

"But the door is closed and we left it open, like we found it." I exclaimed.

"Maybe the wind blew it shut," the sheriff suggested as he pushed it open.

"Be prepared for an awful smell from that room beyond," I warned him. "But that door of that room is open." I was puzzled. "The smell is gone."

We three peered into the room. It had a bunk bed built into the side of the wall. A patchwork quilt covered the bed which was neatly made up.

"This is really weird. I can't understand what that smell must have been." I thought, they'll think I made this all up.

On the ride back down the rocky, dusty road into Tiger and back to the highway, the sheriff told me. "You must have wondered why I wanted to see that cabin, Edna. It seems a sheepherder has disappeared up in this area. No trace of him at all. The owner of the band," he continued, "came up to check on the sheep and couldn't find the herder. He didn't know of any cabin around the area. You see, the herders start below us in Eagle County and keep pushing the sheep up into the high country, over the mountains till they get to Loveland Pass. There they load them on big semi-trailers. He, the owner, found the sheep above Montezuma so the herder had pushed them that far."

I remember having seen herders and their sheep up the Chihuahua Gulch and in the fall, coming down the slopes of Arapahoe Basin. I remembered the ski trail crew up there cooking some lamb stew now and then.

"Well, it might have been a bear in that room, but I doubt it. We'll probably never know what happened to that sheepherder either." The sheriff sounded quite disappointed. "These old mining shafts make wonderful places to lose something if that something is dropped or falls down into one."

The day didn't seem so lovely anymore. I knew I would always wonder what I might have seen had I persisted in getting the door to that bedroom open.

I had not been aware that Summit County politicians were expected to attend all the funerals in the County.

One morning the County Treasurer stuck his head in my office. "Better grab a warm coat, Edna. We're going along with the Assessor and the Sheriff to a funeral."

"Who's the funeral for?" I asked.

"Julius Beckman, one of the Swedes who lived at the old Keystone place."

"That's too bad," I said. "I'll certainly miss that old character."

After the funeral we drove up to Cemetery Hill east of Dillon. I shivered as I stood in the icy wind, wishing I had worn warmer shoes.

While the casket was being lowered, I saw a bottle being passed around the group of mourners. Each took a swig. When the bottle reached me, I noted it was Old Crow bourbon.

Old Crow, I thought. I remembered one evening at the Blue River Inn in Dillon. I was eating supper when the door opened and Julius Beckman entered.

"Evenin'," the bartender greeted Julius, who seated himself at the bar. "What'll you have?"

"I'll yust have some of dat sqvirrel yuice."

"Sorry, Julius, we haven't got any squirrel juice," said the bartender. "How about some Old Crow?"

"Oh, Yesus, no," Julius laughed. "I don't vant to fly! I yust vant to yump around a little!"

When the Affidavits of Labor on the mining claims came due, the miners in the area would come in to file their assessment work. The difference between patented mines and mining claims was that the patented mines had been issued a patent from the President of the United States.

120

These were mines which had been proved bonafide with minerals, and belonged to that person receiving the patent. Sort of like having homesteaded a ranch. The claims, on the other hand, which were on government-owned land, had to have a location certificate filed with map and mining district. The claims only needed $100 worth of work done on each one per year in order to hold the claim.

Therefore, we were swamped with the filing of assessment work which all came due on the first of July. Some of the miners, who came down out of the hills for the first time in months, wanted to make a big day of it.

In the mail one day I received a letter dated March 14, 1949 addressed to me personally. It took me a few minutes to decipher it.

m..r.s. edna.. dercum
summit. county..breckenridge......coliredo

i.tenk.you..four.retunig..of.the.records.and.like..to..
ask.you.wether.you.hewe.some.old.cabins.or.runn.
down.house.around.cocomo.for.tex.ttittle.that.i.could.
by.from.your.county..i.neded.to.
bunk..miners.sence.i.hoping.starth.on.my.prospect.
sune.is.icant.Hawe.olso.ben.wonfdering.weter.you.
possible.havig.some.minig.property.betewen.frisco.and.
cocomo..that.could.be.by.four.tex.tittlle.and.TEKING.
you.AGAIN.And.
HOPING.here.from.you.nick...
babich.leadvile.coliredo

Nick Babich came into the office one day, a tall French Canadian fellow anywheres from 45 to 60 years or more. It was hard to tell the ages of these miners. They walked slightly bent over as if they had been pushing mine carts in and out of a mine tunnel all their lives. Nick had a sweet smile. "I'm filing location on my mine," he told me.

After making out the receipt for it he handed me two dollars more than necessary for the recording. "That's your tip," he said with a childlike trusting smile. He shuffled out of the office before I could return it. Looking at the "location" I noticed he had not mentioned a mining district or attached the necessary map. I wondered if he even knew where it was.

It was the spring of '52. One day Adina and I decided we'd like to enter a slalom race up on Berthoud Pass. We were both working all week but this race was on a Sunday so we could go.

A bit of a blizzard started early Sunday morning, but not enough to discourage us. Piling the kids into her old Studebaker, we headed up over Loveland Pass. About 20 feet from the top the tires started to spin. It just needed a bit of a push. "Just hold the steering wheel steady," we told the two older youngsters. With Adina on one side of the back of the car and I on the other, we pushed it inch by inch to the top. The rest of the way wasn't a problem.

Two days afterward we read in the *Summit County Journal*, "Adina Ganong and Edna Dercum both raced at Berthoud Pass last Sunday, and they both done good." How good we "done" no one but us knew! The day of the race it was cold and blizzarding at the top of the hill where the slalom was to start. We were told there was a gate halfway down where you had to either back in or kick turn to enter the gate. It was between a big rock and next to a sharp drop off. I backed in and Adina kick turned in, but we both "done good" and finished.

After the race there was an awards dinner near Georgetown. We couldn't miss that. We were met at the door by a fellow I'd seen the week before when he was hitchhiking to Dillon. His car had run out of gas about four miles east of Dillon and I had given him a ride into town on my way to work. He was the new owner of this resort. Everything, buffet and drinks, were on the house for us. After the gala party, which the kids enjoyed as much as we did, we put the little ones to sleep in the back of the car. We headed on over Loveland Pass arriving safely home. A crazy day, and a crazy race. We were all pretty much bushed, but, as we reminisced later, we sure "done good."

Sometimes, on Wednesday evenings, I would go directly from the office to Climax to ski. The hill would be lighted until 10 p.m. After an evening at Climax I arrived back at Ski Tip to find the living room crowded with guests. As I stood warming myself at the fire, a young lady came up to me and asked, "What group did you come with?"

"What group did I come with?" I was speechless. That evening, as we were preparing for bed, I told Max, "I'm quitting the office in May. I just made up my mind."

He looked at me thoughtfully. "Are you sure you want to? Remember how much you enjoyed running for the office on your own and winning in this county five to one?"

"That's just it, Max. I'll have to run again this fall and tie myself down to two more years in that over-heated building. Worse than that, I'll lose the summers with the children growing up. I'll only get to ski with them on Sundays. The following election I will be over 40 with the same decision to make. I would begin to feel like a stranger around here."

"Thank God!" Max exclaimed. "It was O.K. when we really needed the money, but now we'll be able to make out just fine. Also, Edna, you'll be able to take the ski instructor's exam this May. Why not quit the first of May?"

So it was all decided. What a release! No more of that drive to Breckenridge every morning.

As I turned over the books, the reins, the responsibilities, to my new deputy, Luna, I couldn't help feeling grateful. Not only had I learned to borrow money, but, best of all, I had become closely acquainted with the mountain people, the miners, the ranchers and the townspeople of this unique and beautiful county. Hopefully I'd learned to respect their straightforward, honest, and fearless way of life.

10

Ski Tip Ranch — Guests, Guests, Guests

Thank God there are still enough of the old timers left to have made running a ski lodge for 25 years a lot of fun. Over the years we have seen the change in guests at Ski Tip Ranch.

The very first guests at Ski Tip set the mood. Skiers were not very clothes conscious in those days. I remember well, the late Fred Iselin, standing in front of our fireplace and saying, "When I first came to Aspen to teach skiing, my ski pants were baggy and my face was smooth. Now my ski pants are sleek and smooth and..."

Most of our guests were wonderful, but even the few exceptions weren't all that bad.

I was still working at the Court House five-and-a-half days a week. In the fall of 1949 a jolly Swiss fellow stopped at Ski Tip. He was looking for a place that would sleep and feed about 10 or 12 skiers over Thanksgiving. We had moved out of the original two rooms of the old cabin and were using the new wing with dining room, kitchen and living room. The big stone fireplace in the living room was all finished. Four large windows at the far end of the living room had no glass in as yet. We had found a substitute we could afford to buy. It was a soft plastic-type material which was used in chicken coops to let in light. By fastening a sheet of this to the outside of the windows and another sheet to the inside, it let in enough light. This gave the room a diffused-light Japanesey effect. When the wind

124

blew, the two sheets would reverberate giving off a drum-like sound.

Hadn't we learned about borrowing money? We could buy 12 army surplus bunks and enough bedding. Six skiers could sleep in each of the two downstairs rooms. We assured the happy Swiss right then that we could take care of the group.

To the bank we went. With the loan we were even able to buy a dresser for each room. We put up hooks for their clothes. The one bathroom we had was next door to these rooms. We were in business, the ski lodge business.

Thanksgiving approached with no group, no word from anyone. We had never thought to ask for a deposit. It had never crossed our minds.

Bestemor was to help me plan the dinner. The evening before Thanksgiving the phone rang. "Could you take in two fellows? We are from London but working in Chicago where we heard your names mentioned at a ski club meeting. If we catch the Burlington Zephyr, then the bus from Denver in the morning, we understand we'll reach you by afternoon." I was nervously awaiting the arrival of our first guests. What will we charge them? I wondered.

Late in the afternoon here came a rental car right up to the back door. "Are you from Chicago?" I asked the two men who got out. "Why yes," they both answered. "Oh, you're English? Come right in." I ushered them through the kitchen and on into the living room.

They looked at each other and smiled. "English? Of course out here I guess maybe we are." I put them in the "men's dorm" and showed them the bathroom.

The two bonafide Englishmen arrived at this moment. I looked at the other two men. "We're not imposters, Mrs. Dercum," said the one whose name was Max. "We just thought that maybe out here we had to be English to get in."

Little did I dream then that these would be the first of many guests who would return season after season. Pat Leigh and John Hogg, the Londoners, came from Chicago every weekend for the entire season. Max Schiff and Jack Witkowsky, also from Chicago, almost as often.

125   The next year John was transferred to the Kansas city office of Lloyds of London. He could not catch a train that would get him into Denver on Saturday morning in order to meet Pat, who arrived from Chicago. Therefore John bought an old car. He would drive at 90 mph all night, arriving at Denver's Union Station in time to meet Pat. They would then drive to Arapahoe Basin. They'd ski like mad all day, come down to Ski Tip to party all evening. Then they would ski all day Sunday, heading back that evening. "The Wild Englishmen" the rest of the guests dubbed them. I was glad I didn't have to see how they looked at their offices on Monday morning. We were sorry to see them transferred back to London, but whenever they returned to the States they would call us and would come by if it were ski season.

A third fellow, Dick Hart, joined Max S. and Jack W. When they were there we had such lively crazy times. Our friendship grew. One time, when we were adding a new wing onto Ski Tip, we needed $3,000 to get it finished. I called Max S. asking for help. To make it all legal here came, from the three of them, separate checks for $1,000 each. There were three notes for us to sign at two percent interest, but no date for payment.

Years later, when our son Rolf was granted a Denver University ski team scholarship, he appeared at the Dean's office. However, his papers did not have the necessary authorization for his athletic scholarship. Willy Schaeffler, who was in Europe at the time, would have to O.K. it, Rolf was told. We knew that as soon as Willy returned, he would sign. But Rolf had to get entered. He needed $2,000 which would be refunded as soon as Willy returned. I called Max Schiff in his office in Chicago and fortunately caught him.

"It's in the mail in ten minutes, Edna. And there won't be any notes to sign. I always told you and Max that if you needed any help for those kids of yours, to just call me." As soon as Willy was back, we refunded the money to Max. No wonder many guests like Max felt they were a part of Ski Tip.

It was often a little complicated, having only the two dorm rooms those first years at Ski Tip Ranch. There were three double-deck bunks in each dorm, one room for girls, one for boys. If couples came, they would just have to split up. Nobody had complained so far. Being among fellow

Max carves our entrance sign

Cozy corner—Ski Tip living room

Guests sing along with Rolf's accordion.

127

Ski Tip Jam sessions in the rathskeller.

"Get to ski school, Max," I threaten. Guest Ken Godfrey referees.

skiers, eating with friends, and talking over the day on the slopes together in the evenings before a big roaring fire, seemed to make up for any short-comings.

There was an exception one day. I was showing a new guest where he would sleep, thinking he'd be pleased to have come early enough to claim a lower bunk. He turned to me and said, "But I've got two hundred dollars on me!"

Just then, a good friend of ours, Harry Baum, strode into the dorm. "I'll take an upper bunk, Edna," he told me. He threw his rucksack up on the bunk. Turning to smile at the other fellow, Harry was as astonished as I was at the man's expression. It was complete fright.

"I can't sleep here," stated the newcomer. "I told you I have two hundred dollars on me." He held his hand over his back pocket. I wanted to laugh, thinking that Harry probably had more than that on him and thought nothing of it. Harry Baum, years later, bought the entire Breckenridge Ski Area!

I put up a cot in our cramped and dusty laundry room for the nervous guest, and was glad to see him leave the next morning.

Curly Mackie, an old miner from Breckenridge, became a part of the Ski Tip staff that first winter. When summer came, he and Max decided we needed more rooms. A new wing was added on the north end of the building. We cut the logs from our own property, all of us helping load them onto the truck, driving them to our little sawmill, and then to the lodge where we would peel them. We couldn't afford to hire the Swedes from Keystone village to square and hand hew them for us. We put up the logs round as they were. My job was to chink these. As the winter wore on, the logs would shrink a bit here and there, away from the chinking. This let into these rooms a little more fresh air, some blowing and drifting snow, and more daylight.

One morning at breakfast, a new guest timidly stated, "My room wasn't very warm," only to be scornfully put down by the rest of the guests. "What do you want? Egg in your beer?" or "How about some pheasant under glass?''

One day a most handsome young man arrived, resplendent in cowboy attire. He announced he had come to stay for two months because he wanted to become a ski instructor. He was a Colorado native, his family had several ranches near the foothills in northern Colorado. He caused quite a stir among the female skiers from Chicago. Ninety percent of our guests came from the Chicago area in those early ski years.

I was the breakfast cook and Don, the cowboy, didn't think much of my pancakes. The following morning he marched into the kitchen and took over. For the next two months he made delicious pancakes. We had apple pancakes, pecan, blueberry, any kind. They were terrific. His first attempt was a disaster. He had prepared the sourdough the night before, and by next morning it had overflowed onto the floor. What a sticky mess!

This started a trend. With handsome Don in the kitchen, we had a problem keeping the female guests out. It wasn't the first or last time guests would take over the kitchen. I remember especially one time in the early days of Ski Tip when I had been over to Aspen to ski and ran into Max Schiff there on the mountain. I had planned to ski until noon, getting back to Ski Tip early as it was my night to cook. With the drive home a three hour one, I was sure I could pick up some steaks in Dillon on the way and still arrive around four p.m.

In my hurry to ski I'd forgotten to pick up an instructor's pass so I looked for an instructor friend. Sandy Sabbatini was in line ahead of Max and me. Telling him I'd forgotten to get a pass, I asked for help. Sandy said that when he was loading his class he would tell the lift loader to let me on. No problem.

We got to Midway where another friend, Bengt, was with his class. Bengt told the next loader to let me on. We skied all morning, hating to stop as the snow was perfect. But all good things must come to an end. I put my skis on the car while saying *auf Wiedersehen.*

Max S. laughed. ''Those lift loaders were so concerned about remembering you were to ride free, that they never once checked me. I had forgotten to get a ticket too."

Back in Dillon, I bought the steaks at the old false-front grocery. John Sondregger, the owner, made sure they were cut just as I wanted them. When I drove up to the back door of Ski Tip Ranch I could see a lot of activity going on in the kitchen. There must have been at least six guests running around.

"What's going on?" I asked. Pretty Hannah Gibbs, who had driven up from Pueblo with her husband, looked up from the chopping block. With the big meat cleaver in her hand she said, "We were afraid you wouldn't get home in time. We found all this frozen hamburger in the freezer. Thought if we chopped it up it would thaw faster and we could have hamburgers. We've got some of the guests setting the table. Peter, here, is peeling carrots and potatoes." Matter-of-factly she started hacking away at the hamburger as bits of it flew all over. I looked at the wall all spattered with meat and couldn't help laughing.

"Stop that, Hannah," I ordered. "We've got marvelous steaks from Dillon and I'll take over. Thanks loads, I really appreciate all this. Please go on in by the fireplace and brew me up a drink. I'll need one. I'll tell you later all about my adventures in Aspen. By the way, Max Schiff sends his best to all of you. He'll be along to ski here in a couple of days." I realized that all my guests knew each other and by now were good old friends, even though they came from various parts of the country.

Not only did the guests help, they also disrupted the kitchen. One evening, after dinner, I was walking by the basement door. Having just left the living room where Max was playing the clarinet to the accompaniment of a guest playing the piano with one finger of each hand, I heard pounding down in the basement. I had to see who was down there in the "Black Hole of Calcutta" as we dubbed it. "Bill Goltra?" I was astounded. "What on earth are you doing down there?"

"I'm rebuilding these darn dining room benches so you don't fall off one end when someone stands up at the other end."

Max had realized he'd made a mistake by building the legs of the benches too close to the middle, but everyone thought it was funny to play "spill-the-new-guest." However, realizing Mr. Goltra was very happy down there, I left him to it. Years later we were invited to visit Bill and Pauline Goltra at their baronial estate outside of Chicago. We were greeted with love and warmth. They came back year after year to the little room in the old wing with the two baths down the hall. They and their two sons became proficient skiers.

One evening during dinner Mrs. Goltra was called to the phone. She returned to the table completely overwhelmed. "It was the Chicago police. They have arrested our Yugoslavian gardener for murder!" I was as astonished as she was. We had seen him when we visited the Goltras, and he had appeared very mild and harmless.

By dessert time someone called Mrs. G. to the phone again. I hadn't heard the phone ring, so was immediately suspicious. I rushed upstairs to my room where there was an extension. My door was open and I could hear a clicking sound. One of our ski-bums, Sue, was holding the phone to her ear as the oldest Goltra son was slowly making the clicking sound with an egg beater held close to the phone. While I watched unnoticed, Sue was saying, "Mrs. Goltra? This is Western Union. We have a telegram for you. GARDEN CLUB TREASURER ABSCONDED WITH ALL FUNDS."

I didn't wait to hear more but rushed downstairs just as Pauline was seating herself again at the table. "I knew it. I just knew I couldn't trust that woman." Looking up at me, she added, "There *is* something fishy going on, isn't there, Edna?"

I invited her upstairs to catch her son and Sue in hysterics with her son still waving the egg beater. Being the terrific sport she was, we all had a great laugh together and with the other guests back in the living room.

Probably the craziest guest antics occurred when we had a group belonging to the Chicago Social Register, complete with their own newswriter from the *Chicago Tribune.*

Some of our old-time Chicago guests were already at the lodge. Before supper I was preparing a tray of hot mulled wine to serve the guests around the fireplace. We had no bar yet at that time.

"I'll do that," one of the old-time guests, Jeanie, said to me as she took the tray from me. "Let me serve them." I followed her into the living room, puzzled at her attire. Usually she was in after-ski clothes which I was sure were from Saks Fifth Avenue. There she was wearing a too-big brown turtle neck shirt (her husband's no doubt), a string of long gaudy beads, and only one long, gold earring. Instead of her well-fitting Bogners, she had on baggy ski pants and very high heeled, black patent leather slippers with sharp pointed toes.

I followed her into the living room where our new guests were seated around the fireplace. All of them were dressed more appropriately for the Astoria than for Ski Tip. As Jeanie approached each guest with the wine, she would announce, "I learned to dress up like this at *Boying* Mountain." Boyne is an expensive ski resort in northern Michigan. Looking up, I saw a young man come trooping through carrying a mattress with four youthful gymnasts following. They laid the mattress on the floor at the far end of the room and preceeded to attempt some tumbling acts.

The fireplace group sat open-mouthed watching these barefooted rascals cavorting. However, the newswriter was grinning and enjoying it all. A couple of weeks after everyone had gone home, Jeanie called from Chicago. "You've got to hear this, Edna!" She proceeded to read from the *Chicago Tribune* society column. It was all about Jeanie and her family, how often they came to Ski Tip, what they wore on the mountain, what a charming place the lodge was, and not one mention of the group with whom the newswriter had come.

Before excellent air connections were common, most guests came by train. They would leave Chicago in the early evening, arrive in Denver around 8 a.m., and catch the 9 o'clock bus up to Arapahoe Basin, arriving there around 11:30 a.m. The eager ones would have changed into ski clothes on the train to be ready to ski the moment they arrived at the ski area, knowing Max and I would be there and could bring them "home." New guests had been told to get off at the foot of Loveland Pass on the west side, cross over to the filling station, and call Ski Tip from there. Whoever was at the lodge would drive over and pick them up. The cook,

Oma, or sometimes a guest who had decided not to ski that day, would happily oblige.

One day around noon when I had stayed home on my day to cook, I heard a loud motor sound coming up our Montezuma road. Being a mile from the main highway, we seldom had any "articulated lorries" (as one of the London guests called them) come by. Here came a big Trailways bus which turned into the front drive, and drove right up to the walk, the only place free of snow.

I was dumbfounded. Surely I didn't take a group I don't remember about, or did I? I tore out to the bus as the driver got out explaining, "I'm bringing you a guest. I've dropped so many of your guests off at Montezuma Road, I just had to come in and see this place." I thanked him. Seeing how this guest was dressed, I realized his special delivery was just as well. Out of the bus tripped a young lady in a swirling satin skirt and golden sandals. The rest of the occupants of the bus were staring and laughing as I helped this young New Yorker into the lodge. She didn't have a bit of ski clothing, not even a sweater. When she left later in the week, I noted that she had written in the guest book, "Thanks for all the borrowed warm ski clothes."

The first time our "Lulu" arrived she kissed her hubby after he'd carried in all her luggage, then waved goodbye to him. She stood for so long in the living room looking around, I wondered what was wrong. "Sweetie," she turned to me, "I'm just casing the joint. That fellow over there, did he come with a wife?"

Telling her of the "happy hour" just about to begin, I got her off to her room, knowing she'd want to dress up for the occasion. Soon, here she came dressed in flowing Pucci evening pants of imitation leopard skin. Stopping dramatically in front of the fireplace, knowing all eyes were on her, she gave a wiggle and said, "Hold that tiger."

"What now?" I wondered. A quiet feline voice piped up at the far end of the room, "I see you've got your tiger rag on." Somehow, I had to blend this group together. How? Someone sat down at the piano and the

134

jam session was on. Instead of a tiger-rag girl, we had Ethel Merman!

A party that went on most of the night was O.K. if all the guests joined in. However, if some guests wanted to sleep, and others carried their fun and hilarity into the late hours, I would march down into the living room and announce, "I've gotta race tomorrow so everyone off to bed." If that didn't work, I would pull the fuse on the living and dining room fuse box and tell them that the electricity had gone out in that wing.

When we had word that eight Texans would arrive by private jet to Denver, and would come up to Ski Tip in two rented station wagons, we assumed these men must be millionaires. One of our ski-bums had taught skiing in New Mexico. "They'll expect the red carpet treatment," she informed me.

"O.K.," I told her, "let's collect all the red towels and red rugs we can find. I've got that old red material we had for drapes years ago in the living room." All tacked together and laid down on the walk from the front door to the parking lot, it made a red carpet of sorts. One of the other ski-bums found some more old material and made the flag of Texas which we hung on the front door.

They arrived in their two station wagons with enough luggage for two weeks instead of two days. They loved the "greetings" and after supper they kidnapped the entire crew. They all moved on down the road to the nearest bar, The Loveland Pass Bar and Lounge.

When the bar closed at two a.m. all of them came trooping back and informed me, "We're all gonna have some scrambled eggs. And, don't you worry, little lady, we'll do the cookin'." No multi-millionaires had ever cooked in our kitchen and I'm sure none have cooked there since. The eggs, which we all enjoyed in front of the fireplace, were delicious.

The next night, we went to bed early, as I felt one night of carousing with the Texans was enough. At two a.m. I was aroused by a thumping and banging of benches in the dining room, which was below our bedroom. Very quietly, I crept down the stairs and peeked around the corner to see what was going on. On the floor was a figure crawling around on all fours and pulling the living room floor lamp behind him. "What on earth are you doing?" I asked him.

He looked over his shoulder at me and I recognized Mr. H. Hunt, Jr., son of one of the richest men in the world. "I've lost my contact lens."

"Look," I said, "that's not the way to look for anything like that! You've got to put your cheek down on the floor." I got down on all fours to demonstrate, and there, glittering in the reflected light from the lamp, was his contact lens! He smiled and thanked me, taking himself off to bed leaving the lighted lamp in the middle of the floor and the tables, benches and chairs all helter skelter. Max slept peacefully through it all. It's a good thing I can hear sounds that go bump in the night, I thought, or that poor

136

man would still be there on the floor when we all come down for breakfast.

I remember one time after midnight when our cook, Hazel, knocked on our bedroom door. "Max, Edna! Wake up! I smell something burning!"

Max was out of bed like a shot, tore down the stairs and down the hall, shouting as he knocked on all the doors, "Everyone up! Fire! Everyone up!"

Having a good nose for smelling out smells, such as leaking gas or smoke, I followed my nose to our daughter, Sunni's room. She had a cold, so I had put a water-filled tea kettle on an electric plate in her room. It had boiled dry and there was our burning smell. I called to Max, "I've found it." He came up and we went back to bed. Luckily, Sunni slept through it all.

The next morning at breakfast, I asked apologetically, "Didn't any of you hear Max yelling up and down the hall last night?" The guests all looked at me with surprise, except one who said, "I wondered who that was pounding on my door before daylight. I thought he wanted to get me up to go skiing on the Little Professor. So I said, 'Nuts to him,' turned over, and went back to sleep."

One year we tried something different. It lasted only three summer months and was a nightmare. We leased a motel.

With the idea of an easier life with no meals, and no cooks, we tried it. Max and Rolf were to stay at Ski Tip and build a new kitchen and upstairs wing. Sunni and I, with the help of a left-over-from-winter ski-bum would run the motel.

Our lease started July first. The owner had assured us that we'd be filled early and really make a lot of money on the July Fourth weekend.

The first night we rented three of the ten units by five p.m., and then nothing. At this point, I must explain the bell system. When we were in the apartment back of the office, we needed to hear the bell ring up front. The owner had rigged up a tin plate over the buzzer of the bell, so when it rang, it literally sent us out of our chairs. After the first three buzzes we felt we'd gotten used to it. Nine o'clock, then ten o'clock came, and no buzzer sounded. I offered to wait up and sent the girls off to bed. Finally, at 12:30, I went to bed after leaving the front office open, the lights on, and the vacancy sign lighted.

I had just dozed off when the buzzer sounded. Picking myself up off the floor, grabbing my bathrobe (I couldn't find my slippers), I tore out barefooted to the cold office. There stood a tired-looking couple with a small baby. It wasn't hard to herd them to a room. Gratefully, I fell back into bed and in five minutes I was fast asleep.

Clang, went the buzzer again. Here was the father of the baby holding out towards me a baby's milk bottle. "I need this warmed for the baby." Like a zombie I went back to the kitchen, heated the bottle, testing it for the right temperature, and handed it back to him. With no thanks he tramped off to his room.

Off went the lights, the NO in front of VACANCY went up, the door was closed and locked, and off to bed I went. "The Fourth of July weekend starts tomorrow," I thought, "and we'll really fill up then." A good night's sleep was all I wanted. On Friday we were all filled up by three p.m. for the next three days.

I was sound asleep the third night when suddenly the buzzer lifted me right up out of bed, horizontally, I'm sure. There was a banging on the office door. I grabbed my robe, tiptoed to the front door, gingerly opening it a crack, and peering out, I saw a vision in a pinky-peach, or peachy-pink. Playboy Bunny, I thought, looking at her through my half-asleep daze. What on earth is *she* doing here?

"Quick!" She pushed by me and slammed the door, locking it behind her. "My husband is going to kill me! He got drunk at the Dillon Rodeo. I took the car and drove back here. We're in unit six."

Dandy, "Peachy," I thought. Right next door! She had a peach-colored shorty nightie, peach-colored fluffy slippers, and peach-colored hair.

"He'll have to walk five miles from Dillon here. Will he be mad, mad enough to kill me! I know, 'cause he's drunk enough."

138

Locking and bolting the inner office door, I led her through the laundry to our apartment and locked that door. Fortunately, there were two beds in my room. I told her she could sleep there.

"Sleep?" she asked. "I can't sleep with him comin' for me."

I took out the heavy Colt automatic Max had left with me and put it in my pocket. It made my robe sag to one side almost to the floor. I looked at my watch. It was two a.m. In the faint moonlight the tree shadows seemed to move eerily.

Peachy sat cross-legged on the other bed staring out the window while regaling me with all her romantic conquests. Five-thirty came. Peachy announced, "He musta come back and went to bed. He'll be O.K. now."

"He won't kill you if you go back in?" I asked. Then I thought to myself, if he doesn't, I will. I let her out and fell into bed for the two hours left to me.

When fall came I returned to Ski Tip, happy we took in only skiers. They didn't mind that we had no TV. They didn't say, "Ya mean, ya ain't got no TAY VAY?"

11

More Guests

Famous (or infamous) guests were often unknown to me. One day in the early 60's, I answered the phone and heard, "This is Spiros Skouris. I am calling from Vail. My wife and I are driving through from Vail with our four children and their French governess. We've been told your place is a fun place to stay. Unfortunately, we can stay only one night as we have to catch a plane for New York in the morning." Assuring him that we could take care of them, I wondered who is Spiros Skouris.

Going into the kitchen, I told my cook and the dishwasher, "Someone with a most unusual name is coming, Spiros Skouris." The dishwasher exclaimed, "Why he's a Greek shipping magnate!"

Luckily, I remembered, we had our very best room with bath available, plus two dorm rooms.

A wild snowstorm developed and I feared they wouldn't get over Vail Pass. After almost giving up on their arriving, a car drove up. I stood at the door to welcome the Skouris family. A handsomely-dressed couple got out. "The others are coming behind us," they told me as they hurried through the swirling snow to the door. I ushered them up to their room. The governess must be driving the other car I decided as I hurried downstairs, just in time to see a big station wagon arrive. Out poured four children and three adults. The man greeted me, "We are the Skourises." I asked puzzled, "Who—who is the other couple? The other couple who arrived just ahead of you?"

"Oh, they're from Grand Junction. We helped pull them out of a snowbank up on Vail Pass!" So, into the two dorm rooms (with baths down the hall) I put the Skouris family and governess. And the blizzard raged on. It snowed for four days. We had a great time with everyone enjoying being snowbound.

One of the Skouris youngsters asked me, "Does the mail really come in by dog sled?" Aha, I thought, the stories the rest of the guests are handing out to the new guests are going along as usual.

Rich or poor, no guest had ever worried about thefts or crime while at Ski Tip, or for that matter anywhere in the area in those days. We didn't either. None of our doors had locks. If we went away, we just went away. Our guests enjoyed this lock-free set up. This way there were no keys to worry about losing. Our car and jeep sat out all year with the keys in the ignition. After all, if one locked up one might forget where he had placed the keys. This also was the case with our skis at the ski area. Often, if I'd decided to take a run at the end of the day, I would find the ski school locked when I got down to the bottom. I would just leave my skis outside of the building and they were always there the next morning.

There was an exception during one Christmas vacation. We had had snow and more snow. I was looking forward to the first day the storm would end and the sun would come out.

A young couple, who had made reservations for the holidays, were bringing their grandmother. She would want a room to herself as "she can afford to pay double occupancy," they told us. When they arrived, she sailed in ahead of them in her full length mink coat. On a diamond-studded leash and following at her heels was a well-clipped black French poodle wearing a diamond dog collar. Looking at this formidable dowager, I expected her to be wearing a diamond-studded dog collar also.

"I've come to watch all these young people ski," she told me. "It's such an unusual experience for me — all this rustic atmosphere."

The storm crescendoed around the lodge. It snowed and snowed and each day the skiers headed up to Arapahoe Basin. The last day of the holidays came. The storm had ended leaving a warm sun, blue sky, and loads of powder snow.

At breakfast I noticed a tight-lipped look on the dowager's face. Putting this down to maybe her usual "day-of-departure" look, I paid no more attention. I had on my ski clothes, all ready for the mountain, when she took me aside, stating in a whisper, "My diamond ring is missing — my diamond surrounded by sapphires."

She took me back to her room, showing me where she had hidden it during the night. "At dinner last night I wore my ring," she moaned, "but I turned it inward so none of the guests would see how big it is." I wondered why she bothered to wear it. She had put it, so she told me, behind the mirror which rested on the dresser.

I asked her, "Behind the dresser? It's probably on the floor." I proceeded to look behind the dresser, under it, under the beds. Seeing the dust, I thought, "I've got to jump on the ski-bums. They've only dusted under her bed, not the other one.

"Are you sure you didn't put it in your suitcase, or make-up box? Maybe it could have dropped into one of these many jars of face cream?" She had an array of bottles and creams, enough for every pore of her face. We looked and looked, but no ring. I hurried back to the living room, just in time to grab the last ski-bum. Pulling her back in by her parka, I told her, "Tough luck, but you're going to help me search for a diamond ring. Have you burned the waste basket trash yet?" She had, and in the fireplace. I told her to start sifting the ashes while I would sift through the vacuum cleaner. Knowing the girls shook the dust mop over the porch stoop outside the hall door, I took Max's crow bar and pried up the front stoop. Nothing. I felt something nudge me. There was the French poodle. I grabbed him, tying him to the door post.

"What are you doing to my darling?" the dowager cried behind me. "Maybe he ate the ring, and maybe he didn't, but I'm going to make damned sure." I looked up at the blue sky, with the blue shadows lengthening as the day wore on. Her grandchildren came and they all soon departed. She had no idea of what she had made me lose — millions of priceless sparkling diamonds to ski through and send flying in the breeze.

Early the next morning the phone rang. As luck would have it, Max

142

answered. I could hear from the dining room. "What's that you're saying? You're sending up a special investigator? What for? We're a bunch of jewel thieves? You've gotta be kidding." He hung up.

Of course, everyone in the dining room could hear. With my telling of it all and my lost day of skiing, they sympathized. Then they hooted with laughter. The ski-bums loved it. "Didn't know we were a bunch of jewel thieves."

"Why," said one in a cockney accent, "I'm a bloody cat burglar."

Needless to say, our present guests would not let this drop. They all departed at the end of the holidays. Early in January, Western Union phoned from Leadville. "Mrs. Dercum, we've got a strange wire for you." She proceeded to read it, "JEWEL THIEVES RELAX, FOUND THE KNIFE.—THE MILWAUKEE GOON SQUAD." She continued, "And here's another telegram signed, The Chicago Syndicate."

The next morning Western Union called with a telegram from Hollywood:

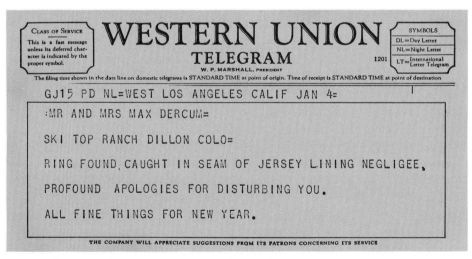

And she hadn't let me search her suitcases!

When the copy of the telegram arrived, I read it with anger. Then I started to laugh, and suddenly felt sorry for her.

Upon awakening each morning, I would tell myself, tonight I will *not* party with the guests, but will go to bed early. This good intention was out the window as soon as supper was over. There was too much fun going on.

One night I remember most vividly when none of us got to bed at all. At least none of the guests, that is.

A French ski instructor came over from Aspen. After a day of skiing, we were all gathered at the long dining room table finishing our dessert when he asked if any of us had ever played the Cardinal Buff game. "We'll have a Cardinal Buff cheese fondue party and rectify your ignorance," he decided. Off to Dillon I drove, to get the necessary ingredients; lots of cheese, French bread, vodka, and bottles of white wine.

Often one or two miners from Montezuma would stop by and entertain the guests with talk of mining in the high country. This evening was no exception. Of the two men who walked in the door, I knew only one. The other man I had never seen before. The miner said, "This fellow is from Hollywood and I thought you folks might like to meet him. He's Lew Ayers and he's interested in some mines around here."

I was thrilled. A real movie star. I had seen him in *All Quiet on the Western Front.*

Before I could tell everyone about the movie star one of the guests came up to him and said, "You're a mining man then, I take it?"

A vivacious and stunning blonde skier asked him, "Are you a skier, Mr. Ayers?" When he shook his head negatively, she whirled around, losing all interest.

I invited them to stay and join in whatever was "cooking." The French chef-ski-instructor had set everything up on the table in the dining room. "To play Cardinal Bluff, spear a piece of bread, dunk it in the cheese and pop it in your mouth. Then you pick up your glass of vodka." (Thank God, the glasses are small, I thought.) "Put your finger to the side of your nose and bounce on the opposite side of your hip on the bench." Of course, as soon as we did it wrong, we had to start all over again.

I felt I'd better escape into the living room or I wouldn't be able to

144

cook breakfast in the morning, let alone be on the mountain to teach all day. Someone had pushed all the furniture in the living room to the sides and had turned on the record player with some nice dance music. Wandering between the two rooms, I asked myself, aren't they ever going to bed?

Three o'clock came. The moon was bright and full. "It's such a brilliant, beautiful night," someone exclaimed, "let's all go skiing on the Little Professor." It being late spring, the Little Professor across from Arapahoe Basin, had been skied quite a bit. Even though it was an avalanche slope, in the early morning after the cold night freeze had settled it, it was considered quite safe. Everyone, or so I thought, took off to drive up Loveland Pass to ski. Max and I gratefully went off to bed to get what sleep was left to us.

Daybreak came and here came the happy skiers none the worse for wear. I marveled at how they could still be so energetic after such a night. "You should have come along, Edna," the vivacious blonde said to me.

"I guess I'm getting old," I answered.

Off in the living room I heard someone yell in response, "When are you going to quit guessing?" As I went back to flipping the pancakes, I thought, I deserved that.

Upon entering the living room earlier I saw the miner and Lew Ayers sound asleep on the couches. After waking them, the miner said to me, "It's not the skiing I couldn't take, it's all this partying that evidently goes with it."

Amen, I said to myself, and added, tonight, I'm going to bed early.

Our register book, which lay on the front desk, seldom had any addresses in it, just comments. Among the usual "Good chow," and "I'll be back," there were others. "May Day." "Better get the roof fixed, Max." "Converted Eastern skiers." "Hills aren't steep enough." I often wondered if Bob Mann, who wrote the last comment, had ever learned to turn his skis. I remember him going straight down the Molly yelling *track* all the way.

One guest only wrote after his name "Brown Sugar." He loved it on his oatmeal. And a Colonel writing, "Old soldiers never die, they just fade away." To which another guest had added, "Old skiers never die, they just stand in lift lines." "Texas was never like this." And a six-year-old who printed on two lines, "I rilly like staying at Shit Tip Ranch." "What hours we kept!" "Itchie-Bon," (whatever that meant). "Broke my leg, still happy." "Hoop-dee-do." "Don't enlarge." "A cake as yummy as the girls who made it." "We'll be back," and under this, "We *are* back." Olympic diving champion, Pat McCormick (1956) placing in our book a picture of her husband, baby, and herself holding her Olympic medals. Pat learned to ski the entire mountain in one day — a natural athlete. It was a rare day, the most pleasurable day I ever had teaching someone to ski.

It's fun to look through this book at the cross section of famous guests staying with us different years. Some were not famous until later, such as Ben Abruzzo and Maxie Anderson (of the first crossing of the Atlantic by balloon), Ernie Blake of Taos Ski Area, Klaus Obermeyer, Toni Woerndle of Red River, the French Olympic champion Charles Bozon, the entire Dartmouth ski team with coach Walter Prager in 1956, Willy Schaeffler and the D.U. team, someone signing as Mohammed ("mo") Alei, and so on. But none were as famous or as well-liked as Henry Fonda. And he came in the summer time when we had no other guests.

Sometimes, guests had problems besides their ski technique. One evening, as we were sitting in a small group around the fireplace, a female guest age about 40 spoke up. She asked of the handsome Austrian ski instructor as he leaned against the stone wall of the fireplace, "You're a man. What do you find attractive about a woman? In other words, what advice would you give me to attract a gentleman of, say 40 or 45?"

He looked stunned for a moment. Then he said, "Buy a sweater two sizes too small."

A few weeks later as we were sitting and talking by the fireplace, the same guest stood up, stretching her arms upward, and turning around, "Do you think this sweater will help me, Edna?" It evidently did. The next year we received the wedding invitation.

A family with four children arrived one day. The wife announced to

146

me, "This is to be my vacation. I intend to spend it sitting in front of your big fireplace and doing nothing. I don't ski, you see. My husband is going to take the children up to the slopes all day. It will be wonderful." Little did she dream what was ahead for her.

The first day all went well. Daddy took the three boys and the four-year-old daughter up the mountain, entering them in ski class. The next morning the four-year-old was running a temperature. Our closest doctor was 35 miles away in Idaho Springs. Of course, the husband and three boys must ski. Over Loveland Pass Mama drove with the little girl. Back to Ski Tip with medications and a steamer.

The next morning one of the younger boys was running a temperature. Over the mountain went Mama. Our cook said she'd keep an eye on the little girl who was propped up on a couch in a sunny corner in the living room. The next morning the second boy, and the morning after that the third boy came down sick. The mother looked sicker than any of them. Finally, the vacation came to an end with Mama dragging herself out to the car, while Daddy was saying, "Boy, this was a great vacation. Never had a better time."

By the fall of 1963 we had a bar in the rathskeller Max had built. My handsome nephew, Peter, agreed to be bartender for a season. He had come out as a 15-year-old to work on a local ranch 20 years earlier, and still felt that he was a true westerner. When lonely females would climb up on a bar stool to ask Pete if he were married, he would answer, "Nope. I'm a maverick running through the prickly cactus." A natural story teller, he always had a good audience around the bar and business flourished.

Showing Peter a letter from Texas one day, I was surprised at how excited he became. "A whole group! That's great. I'll have to stock up on lots of Jack Daniels. Texans really go for bourbon. I'll be ready for them. Why, that large a group will fill up the whole lodge almost. Boy, the bar business will be really great."

So, down to Denver Peter went, stocking up on cases of bourbon. The day of the Texans' arrival came.

Coming home from skiing I found Peter had opened the bar early. He had on his cowboy hat, jeans and boots. "I'm ready for 'em," he grinned.

An entire bus load arrived. As they congregated in the living room and rathskeller, where Peter had herded most of them, he greeted them with "Howdy, folks."

Then I heard a woman say, "Rat friendly they are."

"Step right up, folks," Peter encouraged them. "I know you all must be thirsty after that long drive. Just step right up here to the bar."

"Thanks," said the one who was the spokesman for the group. "Thanks, but we'alls dry."

"I know," said Pete. "That's why I opened the bar early."

"But, we'alls raelly dry," the man answered. "We'alls don't drank."

"You're puttin' me on!" Pete was dumbfounded. "What do you mean, you don't drink?"

"Rat, rat you are. We'alls from the Church of Crast. We'alls don't drank!" I could see Peter sinking slowly behind the bar. After showing them to their rooms, they came back to sit around the fireplace singing hymns.

At dinner that night, they all stood up and in chorus said, "Let's all hear it for the Dercums. Hooray, hooray! Rat nice and friendly folk!"

We had room for only one other guest that night, a writer for a ski publication. He took me aside later in the evening and said, "I was sent up here to do a write-up on your lodge and all the after-ski fun you have. I don't think I can do a story on this group."

"Come back when all the ski instructors are here for the exam in the spring," I told him, "and you'll get all the partying you'll want."

Probably the one time I was really scared at Ski Tip was when Dr. Peter Gray's second son, John, was born. Peter had come out for several years, always bringing a bunch of youngsters, putting them in ski school and watching over them. This one time he and his wife, Carli, had decided to come out even though she was expecting some two months

148

hence. I don't know if she skied that day, but I do know it was my night to cook. I was stirring the gravy when Peter came tearing out to the kitchen. "Carli's time has come!" he said.

I was stunned. "I can't help you. I don't know a thing about delivering a baby."

"I know that," Peter said anxiously. "I am driving her right now to Denver. What I need is a doctor's name so I can call him."

With great relief, Bonnie and I looked up the phone number of an obstetrician who often came to Ski Tip. "Darn," I thought. "Why isn't he here now?"

Peter and Carli made it into Denver just in time. Peter phoned that all went well. The guests with us drank a big toast to the new baby and his parents.

As one guest remarked, "Peter is the kindest man I know. He would probably have opened several bottles of champagne on this occasion." I pretended I didn't hear the champagne hint. But we all agreed, Peter *is* the kindest man we know.

Sometimes we saw our Ski Tip guests in summer. Peak Ten, outside of Breckenridge, had been discovered to have one of the longer and better summer snow fields in Colorado. At least some of our guests had heard this.

One day in mid July 1954 some of our winter guests from Chicago arrived and announced they wanted to ski Peak Ten. We, having a jeep, could drive them up on the old Briar Rose mining road which climbed to almost the base of the snow field.

Soon word got around that we were going up Peak Ten. Harry Baum offered his jeep also, and we had another party of skiers join us. It was quite a climb up the steep part of the snow. I wondered how our low altitude guests would do.

One fellow, climbing eagerly ahead of us, took a wrong turn and reached the peak next to Peak Ten. There was a saddle-like dip between the two peaks. When he finally got to the top of the snow on Peak Ten,

Hank (Henry) Fonda relaxes at Ski Tip after jeep trip with Max to old ghost town of Sts. John.

July 4th ski trip on Peak Ten with Harry Baum, Harry Jr., Jack Witkowsky and Tink Bailey.

150

he announced, "I've climbed two mountains and haven't come down one yet."

We all traversed and climbed while carrying our skis over our shoulders, except one, who decided he'd rather climb with his skis on. He would traverse and kick turn. This worked well until he got to the steeper part where he made a long traverse. Finally, he had to kick turn or continue into the rocks. He started the kick turn, one ski pointed west, the other east. He looked down on the roofs of Breckenridge, 4,000 feet below. With a gasp, he leaned back, his skis shot out in both directions and he found himself sliding down the snow. He had bought a new pair of jeans. He made a furrow in the soft snow, leaving a blue streak of stain down the mountain for 500 feet. With a wet cold rear he said, "I think I'll head back for Chicago and leave my skiing for the winter."

There was one small group of guests I shall never forget, my one and only brush with the underworld. There were five of them, all men. One had phoned the day before to make the reservation.

I glanced out of the office window as a car drove up with five men in it. Only one got out and came up the walk. I started to greet him, but he brushed by me saying, "Just a minute." He walked into the living room, looked around, and then peered into the dining room. I followed close at his heels as he strode into the rathskeller, stood there for a minute looking everyone over, and then strode back out. I was still scurrying along behind him as he opened the front door and beckoned to the other four to come in.

The next morning they took off for skiing, *I presumed.* At the end of the day here they came. First, the one fellow came in, looking around each room before beckoning the others to come in. I went up to him and asked, "Where did you ski today?"

"Oh, ski today?" he seemed confused by my question. "Why, at Vail, Breckenridge, and I guess, Arapahoe," Wow, I thought. How do you do that?

Judy, our pretty daughter-in-law, was helping out at the bar when the

Italian-looking gentleman, tallest of the five, walked over and started a flirtation. He began his conversation, Judy told me later, with, "Do you know what a black mausoleum is?" Judy must have looked puzzled. Then answering his own question, he told her, "It's the trunk of a Pontiac."

Judy wondered. "What's your business? I mean what do you do?"

"Oh," he answered her with a sly smile, "I'm a juice man."

"A juice man? Do you mean you sell orange juice?"

As Judy was pondering this, one of our wealthy Chicago guests walked into the rathskeller. The Italian man muttered, but loud enough for Judy to hear, "We should have a bit of *his* business."

Later that evening Judy related this weird conversation to our Chicago guest and to me. He laughed. "Edna, when they pay their bill in the morning, it will be in fresh new twenty-dollar bills. Do you have any idea who those guys are? That nice article about Ski Tip in the Pontiac magazine *Safari* probably brought them here. But don't worry," he assured me, "having seen Ski Tip, they won't want a piece of this business."

As predicted, the next morning, the fellow paid their account in crisp twenty-dollar bills.

The next summer a Chicago attorney friend of ours stopped by. Still curious about those five men, I showed him the registration book. "All the addresses are freeways," he told me. "The funny thing is, though, their names aren't wholly ficticious. One is complete and the others have only their first names correct. I've seen them in court."

"When the one paying the bill asked me if we did a good business here, I told him, 'I've never lived anywhere where I've been so poor and still loved it.' He had a funny expression on his face, almost envious."

What really puzzled me was that, years later, wanting to show someone else the names of those five, I couldn't find them. The page where they had registered had been neatly cut out.

Summers were for us.

One summer Max built us a sauna. It was great fun running from the sauna and jumping off the little dock into the icy waters of our lake.

One evening, after a sauna, I ran through the bright moonlight to the lake. Just as I dove in, I heard a splash. I couldn't stop in mid air, so I prayed, Oh, my God! Don't let me land on a beaver's back.

Hastily climbing back on the dock I watched the beaver, as frightened as I was, swimming to his house. Cutting through reflections on the moonlit water, he left a silver-edged wake.

In the winter, with the lake frozen, the guests solved the problem of cooling off after a sauna. "What's wrong with the snow?" I quickly bought some bigger towels. No one brought bathing gear to Ski Tip.

For awhile I never realized the nightly show the sauna-taking guests were putting on for the guests watching from the living room windows. One night, hearing hilarious laughter, I went in to watch the show myself.

Unaware of their audience were several fellows jumping and rolling in the snow. Their big towels were wrapped around their waists and pinned with big safety pins. Now, heavy and wet with the snow, the towels began to sag and slip down till they hung from their hips.

"Oh no," said one of the audience. "We were out there just now, too. We must've looked like those guys. Like a bunch of Indians getting ready to storm the fort at dawn."

It was one a.m. and I was sound asleep in our bedroom upstairs. The head of our bed was against the wall which backed onto the living room fireplace.

Suddenly, I was awakened by sharp and loud hammering right near my head. Wondering what was happening, I hurriedly threw on a robe and rushed downstairs.

Peeking around the corner into the living room, I saw Max and some of the guests looking up to the top of the fireplace.

"Hi, Mom," Dale Gallagher, our local Forest Service ranger greeted me. He was practically upside down and suspended from ropes near the peak of the roof.

153

"I'm showing your guests how to climb a rock face. Now, I'm going across the ceiling over to those beams. We're pretending this is an overhanging rock up here."

I watched in fascination as he proceeded, like a human fly.

Dale, with another mountain climber, had just returned from completing a new ascent of Devil's Tower in Wyoming. *LIFE* magazine had published photos of these two men, dressed in white to show up better, as they made the ascent of the vertical rock face of this dramatic tower.

The pitons are still firmly in place in the stones of our fireplace and across the ceiling. No one since at Ski Tip has had the courage or the expertise to attempt *the climb*.

In going over my notes on guests, I sometimes shudder or laugh. There were so many great times and funny things happening in between the worrying times. Such as the plumbing not working when we used the old two-seater privy back of the old cabin for the emergency, the well going dry, or the guests all getting sick after drinking the "glug" the ski patrol had brewed over an open fire they had built outside the old cabin. They had heated the brew in a brand new galvanized garbage can they had just bought.

I look back and can see myself chasing guests' kids away from taking apart my antique Seth Thomas clock. Or the guest I surprised in the middle of the night down in the rathskeller, shouting and swinging our double-barreled shot gun, vintage 1830. He said to me as I took it away from him, "I swear I heard a burglar down here."

"Well," I informed him, "you could hit him over the head with it. That's all you could do with that gun. I doubt it's been fired since before the Civil War."

The end of spring skiing would come and with it a wonderful day. I would march around to the front of Ski Tip and *KICK* the front door shut.

"We're closed! Closed for the summer!" Yet knowing that come fall and the first snowflakes, I'd be looking forward to the next ski season with Ski Tip full of another Pandora's Box of winter guests.

12

"I Have My Reservations."

Through the years of running Ski Tip as a ski lodge, we had added on a wing here, a few years later another wing there, and a larger kitchen, then a larger dining room, another wing, and so on. During those years we increased accommodations for guests from 12 to 70. In the earlier years with fewer guests we had more time to enjoy them. The later guest-filled years, to be honest, were still years of many pleasures.

"I got a letter in the mail today," I told Max worriedly. "It's a request for 80 reservations! But they state they need only 37 single beds!"

I wonder how they're figuring? I worried to myself, let's see, — 37 single beds leaves 43 people — if they mean 24 more couples. But, that leaves one left over. Maybe he's a traveler. Maybe he comes and goes. Anyway, I won't worry about it. We can't accommodate as many as 80.

Max laughed at my muttering. "Leave me out of this. It's your department. I'll fix the plumbing, cut the firewood and build the fires."

"You will? I mean right now? I mean fix the plumbing right now? In the old bathroom some youngster put his mother's face cream jar down the toilet. She got it out, but now the toilet's got a leak on the side. When you flush it squirts out a stream of water."

Max hurried down the hall. After a few minutes he returned. "I found an empty number ten fruit can in the kitchen and put it on the side of the toilet to catch the squirt. Just keep an eye on it until I get back from ski school. Then I'll see if I can fix it." With that he left and I picked up the ringing phone.

156

"I'd like reservations for my wife and me," the voice said. "There will be 14 children." When he heard my gasp, he continued, "Oh, I'm sorry. Meant to tell you we're four couples." "Glad to know," I answered with relief.

For one who hates to write letters, it is especially hard to correspond with perfect strangers. Every letter to Ski Tip deserved, I thought, a friendly and newsy answer. I felt I should tell them how much snow we had, how good the skiing was, and describe the beauty of the mountains. Maybe it was all to the good that I did write this way, as many guests told me they just had to come to Ski Tip to meet the nut who wrote those letters. One family, from as far as the Port of Spain, Trinidad, told us that they chose Ski Tip because of the friendly and crazy answers to their inquiries.

In the first years at the lodge, I tried to keep the number of guests arriving, their date of arrival, and of departure in my head. With accommodations for only twelve guests, it wasn't too hard to do. If a guest or two were lost in my memory, we would send them down to Oma's house nearby. She told me one day that if I continued doing that she would have to begin calling her place "Ski Tip West."

Luckily, about three years later, Alice Winslow McDonald arrived. Alice became one of our closest friends. We soon accepted her as one of the family, and still do.

Alice had left her job in Denver at one of the large hospitals. After staying a weekend as a guest, she returned and announced she was going to be a ski-bum the rest of the ski season. Having discovered my lack of charts, she brought along a bunch of hospital assignment sheets. We were now better organized with these sheets hung on the wall next to the phone. After that, I was initiated into what I called "my human chess game." I was now able to move the guests around on the chart before they arrived, instead of greeting them at the door and wondering where I would put them.

No two letters were the same. Soon as I got to thinking I had all the answers, along would come a different question. "Do you have skiable snow by Thanksgiving?" No problem there, but the letter would end

Winter

Rolf Dercum

In the brittle cold
   life stands still on a winter morning
The tracery of willows
   etched against the dark intense
   blue green of spruce

The sharp crack
   of a frozen branch
   breaks the breathless silence
Ice crystals
   diffuse the early light of day

with, "Do you think you could find us some good grade sheep? Or find a rancher who would ship us some?"

Then another letter would come along. "Some of us want to come out, maybe March, maybe April. Do you have room? And, by the way, maybe there'll be two couples of us or maybe ten of us, or maybe just me. Do you have room?" I answered that one easily, "Maybe we have — and maybe we haven't."

While I was County Clerk, Max often answered the letters those first years. Neither of us kept carbon copies. When it came to billing the guest we couldn't remember if we'd quoted a rate. Our standard price was $3.75 for lodging, breakfast and dinner. But, sometimes a guest would pull out Max's letter to him. I would read, "We serve breakfast and dinner. Lunches may be obtained at the Basin shelter. Hence, we will deduct 50 cents from the price of $4.00 quoted." "So, it's $3.50, Mrs. Dercum." Of course, I then assured the guest it was. We sometimes felt embarrassed at charging that much!

I soon realized my letters required a map of how to get to our place. Often guests had become lost. They would miss the turnoff west of Idaho Springs and find themselves driving over Berthoud Pass to Kremmling. They would then have to drive 45 miles back south to Dillon and east to Ski Tip. This would be a drive of at least three to four times the distance of coming over Loveland Pass.

One guest never did find Ski Tip, even though he did go over Loveland Pass. He gave up and drove on west. "Even though it was snowing and blowing pretty hard," he wrote us later, "I couldn't resist the temptation of getting out of my car at the top of the pass. After rubbernecking around, I can honestly say I don't remember ever before having seen a more enthralling and perfect ski terrain. I believe I know where you are, but must have missed your place as I drove on down maybe ten miles or more. I came," he continued, "to an antique horse-drawn hearse in front of a log hotel called Wildwood. Is your ski cabin near this? It started to snow so heavily and I didn't have your phone number, so I gave up."

Besides a map, I began to see I'd better put down our phone number too, and make carbon copies of our correspondence.

Some of the letters left me completely confused. This one for instance, "I'm thinking of taking a ski trip to the west this year, but at the moment it is not certain, that I, or anyone else, will make the trip. I hope that someone will be fortunate to make the trip." Or another one, "My mother-in-law will not require the room. However, please reserve both beds you have in this room for my son. He will figure out who sleeps where when he gets there." Or, "Our son Jimmy cannot come, but his brother, John, will take his place, as will the next in line, Frank, who is inseparable from his brother, Jimmy. So, there will be five of them, two boys and one girl. So glad the skiing is good." Or, "I feel quite sure there will be no problem in filling our reservation for ten couples. We may not know what the mix will be, but hope for the best. We enclose a couple of our four-year calendars. Kindest regards." This one had a postscript. "P.S. I have been calling all over the U.S., but I keep losing ground all the time." This P.S. really puzzled me. I decided I'd just ignore it.

It was hard to answer the letters, especially in the evening, with music, laughter and ski talk drifting my way from the living room. A sympathetic guest would wander into the office. "Come on out, Edna, and join the fun." I didn't need much urging. However, after succumbing that evening, and the next, and the next, I was very soon days behind in my letter writing. Not only that, but more letters had come in and piled up on my desk. One January 19th I typed, "Your letter of December 5th certainly deserved a more prompt answer and I apologize. But, the skiing was just too good." Needless to say, I never heard from them again.

Either we hire a desk clerk, I decided, or maybe one of our ski-bums would like to make a little extra money and do the letters in the evening after work.

One of the girls said, "I'd love to do it, Edna. I can type the letters after waiting tables in the evening." What a relief! There was one drawback, however. Our room was over the office then, and our ski-bum, coming in from a late date, would begin her typing. We finally got accustomed to the staccato sounds as she attacked the mail at one a.m.

159
After reading the replies to her letters, I began to realize I had better

proofread her letters before she mailed them. To one of her letters came the answer, "We don't understand. You write you are reserving for us a room with path! Don't you have indoor plumbing?"

A few times, when I was off to the races, I'd inveigle my nephew, Peter, to take over collection of the bills. He offered to do this in the mornings as he was quite busy bartending evenings. I hadn't realized that throwing any figures at Peter would send him into a mental freeze. Luckily, at the bar, the guest just signed a tab, which we'd attach to the bill. After returning home I would often find a note from a guest who had checked out. "By now, Peter will have told you he couldn't figure out my bill, so, I told him you'd calculate it and send it on to me."

Peter had so many other talents. He was a natural storyteller, a popular bartender, an excellent illustrator, but he hated figures, unless they were lovely feminine ones.

One of the most wonderful things, to me at least, was that Ski Tip became financially able to hire a full-time reception clerk, plus two cooks. I realized that I'd always disliked handing a bill to the guests who had become close friends. It was like charging someone we had invited to our home.

Reservations came in regularly, mostly as a result of word-of-mouth recommendations, proving that our unbusiness-like methods at Ski Tip might be inefficient, but our ski lodge was unique and popular.

13

Cooks and Ski-Bums

It was the Christmas of '49 when I finally woke up to the fact that we needed some help in the kitchen. But that cost money which we lacked.

After that fiasco of the group that never showed up, and the bunks and bedding we'd bought going unused, we decided to draw up some rates. Is $3.75 a night, including breakfast and dinner, too much? I pondered. I'll ask my friend, Helen Rich. She knows what's reasonable. If not, she can find out through her job in the Welfare Office.

Since Helen had asked me to give with the scuttle-butt, "in one ear and out my typewriter," I figured her other ear would be sympathetic to my problems.

"Helen," I asked, "what would you do in my place? I'm working here as County Clerk six days a week and driving 20 miles both ways. I really look forward to skiing on Sundays. However, after feeding our friends, ski patrol, and weekenders who pile into our house and ask to sleep in sleeping bags on our living room floor, it's too much. They are great friends, but as soon as they've eaten breakfast, which I cook for them, off they go."

"By the time I get the dishes done," I continued, "I get up to the mountain at noon. Max helps with breakfast too, waiting tables, but he has to be up at the area in time to run the ski school."

"You need to tack up rates on the front door," Helen advised me. "Maybe $3.75. How about $3.50? It sounds better. Then you can afford to hire a cook."

Immediately I shopped around Breckenridge and Dillon for a cook. I was told I might get one for 50 cents an hour. But, I only needed one for weekends. No skiers came up in the middle of the week. I couldn't find anyone.

Then Bestemor came to the rescue. "I'll cook for you," she said. "They'll like my Norwegian lefsa and my good hot oatmeal breakfast." The skiers, who were willing to pay $3.50, enjoyed her as much as her food. Sometimes they would come down early from skiing to help her peel potatoes and carrots. They would sit around the cast iron wood stove in the kitchen listening to her stories while eating her homemade cookies.

Toward spring, Bestemor decided to visit her family in Norway which she hadn't seen for 45 years. Off she went in early March, but before she left she suggested a friend of hers.

Up the road toward Montezuma in our old Alhambra cabin lived a miner (49er) with his 200-pound cheerful wife, Fawntella. On her walks Bestemor had struck up a friendship with "Fawn," as we soon called her.

I did some quick figuring. If we had ten guests on weekends at $3.50, that would be $35.50. I could pay Fawn $4.50 per day leaving enough for groceries. Such things as light, heat, taxes, and repairs never entered our heads. After all, we lived there too. If guests came during the week, which was rare, they would heat up some canned soup and make their own beds. Some even mopped the kitchen floor.

After the ski season we really looked forward to summer. Spring? What was that? The aspens burst into leaf after the last willow-bender, usually around June 11th, which was Bestemor's birthday. On the first birthday she spent in Summit County I remember her saying, "I had to live 70 years before I celebrated my birthday in winter."

When summer did come, it was building time. From Breckenridge came a miner and neighbor of Helen Rich. Curly Mackie had a true Scot's generosity. Mining had come to a standstill. Curly would say, "There ain't two lunch pails goin' out of Breckenridge these days."

It was wonderful mutual help, having Curly there that summer. He had room and board and a rocker in front of the fireplace. Evenings he

162

would sit and rock while listening to Max read to the children. Rolf and Sunni preferred Max's reading to them. At the office we had no duplicating equipment so I had to type everything and then proofread it. After months of proofreading I found myself unable to read stories aloud. I found myself reading like this, "Cap Luck of cap Roaring cap Camp com by cap Brett cap Hart point."

Curly and Max built a sawmill. Their plan for the summer was to build a wing on Ski Tip.

I must explain here how Ski Tip got its name. We had no door knobs on the doors. They were hard to find and expensive when we found any. Since all skiers had wooden skis in those days, we would come across broken ski tips on the mountain, left there by some hapless skier. After discovering how well they worked as door handles on the front door, which had been beautifully carved by Max, we became scroungers of broken ski tips. Our guests donated any they would find on the mountain and soon all the doors had ski tips as door pulls. None of the doors locked, of course, but who worried about that? After suggestions for a name for our place, such as Stagecoach Inn, or Beaver Meadows Lodge, Sunni said one day, "Mommy, we've got so many ski tips around here, why don't we call our place Ski Tip Ranch?"

The sawmill was put up near the old wagon road and ready to go. But it needed logs. On Saturday afternoons and Sundays I would help Max with loading of the logs which he and Curly had cut on the place. Sometimes our good friends, Bill and Jean Bullard, helped load the logs on the truck, using the cat and an A-frame such as Max had used during the war. At the sawmill the logs were slabbed-off on three sides. This made a tighter fit and required less chinking. It also made a flat wall on the inside of the rooms of the new wing, yet left a rounded log wall on the outside. The new wing gave us four rooms downstairs and two rooms upstairs, plus a storage room.

"We must have a balcony," Max decided, and went about carving the boards for it. I offered to paint it with Pennsylvania Dutch designs. I never thought to trace out the designs and paint them on the boards before we nailed them up. We didn't have a ladder long enough for me to reach up and paint the designs. I found it was easier in the long run to hang over the balcony railing and paint the designs upside down. Rain, wind, and snow soon blended it all together. The weathered designs still show colors and nobody seems to know or care what they were.

Another winter was coming. Fawn and her husband had moved away to the western slope where I heard she was cooking at a ranch in the Sweetwater Country. Lucky Sweetwater people, I thought.

Helen Rich came to the rescue again. "Try asking Etta Hooker," she said, and I did. Another lucky day. Etta said she'd clean and make beds, besides cook, and asked only 50 cents an hour.

Business boomed after we posted a brochure at Arapahoe Basin ski area. We were able to pay her, and we all ate well, with Etta happily singing at her work.

We were all set for the Christmas holidays, or so I thought. Etta got the flu the week before Christmas. I was able to find a girl to help, but found no cook. The biggest snow storm of the season began. The guests arrived just ahead of the storm. It snowed and snowed and snowed. Each morning I would start out for my office, leaving Rolf and Sunni with friends in Dillon. Before departing I would put the roast for that night's dinner in the oven, turn the flame low, and pray it wouldn't be all burned up before I got home. We had acquired a small gas stove by then besides the kitchen wood range.

Most of the guests had been at Ski Tip earlier and thought it funny that I was the cook. In desperation I had put up a sign on the door between the dining room and the kitchen:

NOTHING CLUTTERS UP A KITCHEN
LIKE A BUNCH OF GUESTS WHO PITCH IN

The sign didn't do any good as they felt I must be lonely out there. With a drink in one hand, often a cigarette in the other, while leaning against the refrigerator, especially when I needed something from it, they would regale me with their day's skiing. Somehow dinner got on the table. Afterwards some of the guests would line up to help dry dishes. I couldn't wash them fast enough to keep up with them. With perspiration

164

pouring down my face I would hear the last "helper" in line say, "Isn't it wonderful how fast it goes when everyone pitches in?"

I especially remember one guest that holiday. She arrived wearing a mink coat. Her husband and two sons followed with all the luggage. Before I could even greet them she asked, "Is Jimmy So and So here yet?" He was. What complicated matters for her was that he'd arrived three days earlier, just long enough to fall in love with a pretty 20-year-old guest who had the most beautiful golden hair I'd ever seen.

Each evening, after dishes were done, I would sit in the living room, as a hostess should, but longing to be asleep in my bed. Here would come our new mink-coated ,guest, dressed for the evening in flowing silk and wearing silver slippers. She would plant herself down on the couch next to me and in a hoarse whisper, so as not to be overheard, say, "Look at them over there! Playing records! That little blond is nothing but a husband-hunter. How can he fall for her?" I realized that all the time she meant, "Here I am, only in my early forties, sophisticated..."

I was nodding my head sleepily, she thinking I was agreeing. I was only hanging on with my finger nails to keep from toppling over with sleep and boredom.

This was the holiday when I found out the weather decided much of our lives. The day after Christmas came. After breakfast, everyone was saying goodbye. Max, with embarrasment, had collected all their bills which he had laboriously made out. I know the guests often wondered why, when they paid Max, he'd run down into the basement. There we had a small safe in back of the furnace where we "cached" our money.

That morning looked innocent enough. Everyone took off for skiing until two, when they would head for Denver to catch the Burlington Zephyr back to Chicago. I took off for the Court House, which was beginning to look like a sanctuary to me.

Upon returning home and driving into the yard, some of the cars looked familiar. There were several new ones parked in the drive. Going quietly in the back door, I peeked into the living room to find that everyone to whom I'd said goodbye that morning had returned. And, the room was filled with new guests! The long refectory table was loaded

165

with bottles, mixes, ice and glasses. Someone spotted me peering in the door. "Come on in, Edna. We're all back and we are in a party mood." I could see that easily enough.

"The Seven Sisters slid at noon," someone informed me. "All your new guests got in this morning before the slides closed Loveland Pass. We can't get out. What fun. We're snowbound!"

"Where on earth am I going to put all of you to sleep? I haven't got enough beds for all of you." "Oh, don't worry about that," they assured me. "We'll sleep on these couches." One added, "I don't even mind the dining room table."

Luckily, snowplows cleared the Seven Sisters avalanche the next day and things returned to normal, sort of. Max and I decided what we really needed was a live-in cook. Etta was still sick with the flu. She informed me that she and her husband had decided to move south for the winter.

New Year's Day dawned that year with my realization that the one ski-bum I had to help had had to leave the night before in order to get back to school. After the guests had gone, I started down the hall to do the beds. On each door, where the rates had been posted, they had been changed. Upon opening the doors, I found all the beds made and the used sheets and towels piled in a corner. The guests had raided the linen closet. While I was cooking breakfast they had done all this. They had added $2.00 to our rates! Later in the living room I found a letter signed by all of them. "We want to keep coming back, Edna and Max. You won't be able to stay in business unless you raise your rates. We wanted to make sure, so we raised them for you."

About a week later I returned from work to find a couple sitting in the dining room talking with Max. "I want you to meet your new cook," and Max introduced Lena. "This is her husband. He works at the mine up at Climax. Since she's a cook and they need a place to live, it should work out." I was elated.

The next morning, Lena had a delicious hot breakfast ready for all of us. I was surprised to see her wearing a faded flowered bathrobe and dirty floppy bedroom slippers. Well, I thought, no guests, and she's just gotten up. Push away that critical feeling, Edna, she'll be *all right.* I left for work.

166

After picking up Rolf and Sunni at school, I got home at almost six o'clock. A car with Wyoming license plates was parked near the front door. Guests? I wondered. We entered the kitchen where wonderful smells assailed us. But Lena was still in the same bathrobe and was wearing no slippers at all. I looked at her dirty, bare feet.

Lena smiled happily at me. "Got two guests," she informed me. "Two fellas and I put 'em in the dorm. Supper'll be ready at six so get a move on."

Speechless, I rushed upstairs. How will I tell her? She's so cheerful.

"Supper," I heard her call. Coming into the dining room to seat the guests, I saw her seated at the head of the table, still in her bathrobe and bare feet. "Well, set up folks and set to!" Her husband, who was seated next to her on her left, gave her a slap on her arm. "Shut up, bitch, and set to yourself."

I looked at Max, as silent and red-faced as I, and at the two guests who were just as embarrassed.

The next day at the office I thought of ways I could diplomatically approach our new cook. I could see her as I'd seen her when I left that morning. Her bedroom slippers were sticking out from under the stove, and she was still in the sleazy robe. I've got to find a way to ask her to dress as a cook, but I've got to do it so she won't quit.

Somehow I got through the day. I approached home and the kitchen door with butterflies in my stomach. I felt even worse as I viewed several cars in the parking area with Denver rental plates.

Opening the kitchen door, I couldn't believe my eyes. Here was Lena in a neat white uniform, with clean white shoes on *those feet!* She didn't smile a greeting, but looked at me and said through tight lips, "Your mother-in-law arrived today. 'We dress for dinner here,' she told me." Little Oma had had no qualms at all about doing what I'd been dreading all day.

The rest of the season progressed with a trim neat Lena cooking excellent meals for all the happy guests. She and her husband resigned themselves to eating in the kitchen as our new dishwasher also preferred to do. Horatio, a would-be ski instructor, thought he knew the last word on skiing. He had applied for the job, as it left him free to ski all day. "By eating in the kitchen," he said, "I can keep up with the dishes and get out earlier in front of the fireplace. I can listen to them damn skiers talk about how good they are. I could tell 'em a thing or two about how to ski." After watching him on skis I certainly hoped he never got the chance to tell them on the slopes.

Summer and fall went by. Lena then informed me that her husband had gotten another job far away. Back to looking for another cook.

Helen Rich came up again. This time she found us Hazel. Her name reminded the guests of the Hazel cartoons. I remember someone saying, "Ski Tip not only has its own Horatio, it has its own Hazel."

Hazel was a gem. She was also a marvelous cook. The first year Hazel was with us, I found the only hard thing was going to Breckenridge each day to fetch her. She lived there with her family. Each morning I would get up extra early and drive the 20 miles to Breckenridge, dropping the children off at school in Dillon on the way. Arriving home in the evening, I would eat supper with the family and guests. I would then drive Hazel back to Breckenridge, returning home dead tired. All this contributed to my decision to quit my job.

Hazel dubbed Ski Tip "Confusion Lodge." She would call out to me as I left in the morning, "How many for dinner?" I would call back as I was getting in the car, "Let's see — 14? No, drop four. No, wait a minute, I believe it's nine." She would laugh and go back inside humming happily. Actually the best count, Hazel said, was for breakfast, when she checked the row of guests' ski boots on the beams and divided by two.

One day, as our pretty ski-bum, Nora, was showing a guest to her room, I heard the guest ask, "I heard the cook say, 'confusion lodge,' why is that?"

Nora laughed, "Oh, it seems confusing, but it's planned that way."

Hazel was with us for two more years. She was temperamental as are all cooks, I was to learn. One day, after returning from Denver with the crates of lettuce, eggs, and meat for the week, and fighting a blizzard over Loveland Pass, I got home an hour after dinner had begun. I could hear the guests enjoying the dinner while Horatio and I unloaded the car.

168

169

As soon as I entered the kitchen, Hazel threw down her apron and said, "I quit!" She continued in a shaking voice, "If you can't get here in time for dinner, I quit." It took a bit of apologizing and a vivid description of my trip over the pass before she simmered down. All of a sudden, I realized that her temperamental outburst was a relief of worry. I was amused, as I had gotten used to driving that pass. After all, we drove within two miles of the pass every day to go skiing at Arapahoe Basin.

I lost Hazel too, when she and her family moved away. This next time I was lucky in finding Petunia. She was jolly, fat, and loved pink. She had a long, long trailer painted pink which she insisted had to be moved up to Ski Tip Ranch. She wanted it placed right at the kitchen door. We argued with her that if we put her trailer near the old barn, she would have a better disposal system as she would be right over the septic tank. Max found a bunch of the slabs out at the sawmill and built a fence around three sides of the trailer. The barn hid it from the road on the north side. She moaned, "Nobody can see my beautiful trailer."

Max placated her, "But Petunia, I did this to keep those cold winter winds away." Everyone was happy and there was no transportation problem.

With every new cook, one waits with trepidation. Everything seemed perfect with "Pet" as we all soon called her. We now had three ski-bums, plus a dishwasher, and Pet loved them all. Sometimes, as I passed through the kitchen, I would see her recipe book on the table, open at a luscious-sounding dessert. On a piece of paper laid across the page would be written, "Pet! Do It!"

One thing Pet loved to do was to answer the phone, even when she was cooking. As soon as the phone rang she would yell at one of the girls to stir the gravy or watch what was cooking so it wouldn't burn. The phone was located in the living room behind the fireplace in a little closet. Elbowing everybody out of the way, even any guests, she would tear out to the living room. Reaching the phone she would lift the receiver and say, "Ski Tip Ranch. Waddya want?"

It took quite awhile before I realized she was steaming open the letters. Since we were all gone when the mailman left the mail out in the box

170

on the road, she had ample time to do this. After getting home from ski school, I would go through the mail to check on any reservation letters. After all, this was our bread and butter. One day, as I was going through the kitchen, so I could grab some of her cookies on my way to the dining room, Pet called after me. "You got a $200 deposit in the mail today."

I stopped dead. "Pet, how do you know this?"

She was all confusion. "I, I ah, I held the letter up to the window and I could see through it."

I went on into the office, held the letter up to the light and couldn't see a thing through the envelope. Then I realized she'd been opening our mail. "She's a darn good cook and so good hearted. I'd better leave well enough alone," I told Max.

Pet also loved to stand in front of the fireplace, watching the guests arrive. This didn't bother us, only I wished she wouldn't lift her skirt up in the rear to warm her fanny as she stood there.

Pet had a desire to learn to ski. One day Oma, who was then over 80 and a careful snowplow skier, told her she would teach her. Up to the Basin I drove them. Pet had improvised an outfit. She had on heavy wool pants and an oversized red, orange, and black lumber jacket. We finally got her on a pair of skis and told her to stand still in front of the ski school while we put on our skis.

Undaunted, Pet must have decided she could at least walk on the skis. Pushing herself off with her ski poles, she started to slide. I heard a yell and looked up just in time to see her heading for the melted snow patch which had made a small pool of water on the slope in front of the ski patrol building. She swayed back and forth, gathering speed, until she skimmed off into the water and sat down with a big splash! I was laughing so hard, as was everyone else, that I couldn't move. The ski patrol extricated her from the shallow pool.

Gathering what dignity she could, Pet announced, "I was goin' real good until that durn pool of water got in the way."

It was this incident which made me realize how foolish it was for the cook to ski. A new rule went up in the kitchen, "No cook skis except in the off-season." Except Edna.

171

Pet used to threaten to visit the guests at their homes. "You know, Edna," she would say to me. "You wouldn't know they're rich. Why they're real nice. They're real common."

Pet decided one spring, after being with us for several years, to visit a sister in California. She never came back, but had her trailer moved out there.

Back to the newspaper ad search. I'd never asked cooks for references, which this time was a mistake. From Wyoming came an answer, and it sounded great.

She arrived with canary in a cage, a yappy little dog, which our husky, Kiska, could have devoured in one bite, and a cigarette hanging from the corner of her mouth. We were already too close to the start of the season for me to change my mind. Also, after the first two days, we discovered she could really cook.

However, we all missed the happiness in the kitchen, especially the two ski-bums and the dishwasher, who'd come back for another season. "Compared to last year," one of them said, "it's like a morgue in the kitchen." But, she was clean, efficient, and a good cook, so, we all stuck it out.

Once in awhile I did notice when I came into the kitchen that she acted strangely, giving me a squinted look out of one eye, the other closed. I thought nothing of it until one evening when our usually happy and bubbly ski-bum, Bonnie, came running to me in the office in tears. There was a red streak down her cheek.

"She slapped me! That bloody cook slapped me. She's mad because the dishwasher hasn't shown up."

I went into the kitchen to see if I could smooth things over. The cook looked up at me, squinting out of the one open eye. She was picking up the roast which had fallen on the floor. She then bent over and picked up a green pea from the floor and dropped it into a pan on the stove. I saw frozen peas all over the floor. I watched her in horror as she picked up one pea at a time and dropped them into the pot.

Then I realized, she's drunk. But how and where did she get anything to drink? I remembered that some guests had bottles of their

172

own liquor in their rooms, where they'd often have a small party of their own. I quickly made my exit as the other ski-bum said quietly, "We'll get supper on the table, Edna, and then get her to bed."

"Where's the dishwasher?" I wondered. I knew he had been skiing up at Arapahoe during the day. That's all I need, I moaned. Bonnie in tears, the cook drunk, no dishwasher, and a full house of guests.

After things quieted down in the kitchen, and the cook was put back in her room, I plunged in and washed the dishes. Ten o'clock came, ten-thirty. The living room door opened and one of the ski instructors came in to see if any "hanky-panky" was going on, a favorite expression of his.

"Have you seen our dishwasher?" I asked him. "He hasn't shown up at all."

"Oh," he said nonchalantly, "I saw him over at the Red Ram in Georgetown with a good-lookin' blond. I asked him, 'Aren't you supposed to be at Ski Tip?' He was a few sheets to the wind, Edna," he continued, "but he answered me all right. He said, 'I've got those people at Ski Tip wrapped around my little finger.'"

Going to bed that night I was steaming. Hearing the dishwasher drive in around one a.m., I knew what I'd be doing the next morning. I'd be not only firing the cook, but the dishwasher besides. I thought, this is the first time I've fired anyone, anyone in my whole life. I also knew I'd be waking up to the fact that I would again be the cook.

The season was close to the end anyway. The renewed laughter in the kitchen was great, so great, we had a hard time keeping the guests out.

The next fall it was back to newspaper want ads. This time I would request references.

Fortunately, one of our Denver guests dropped by in late summer. I mentioned to her my problem of finding a cook.

"You should screen all the applicants," she told me. "Since I work in Denver, I'll have them meet me there and screen them for you." Being a buyer for a big department store, I knew she'd had experience interviewing people.

It wasn't long after the ad had been in the Denver papers that she called me. "I think I've found the perfect cook for you, Edna. Get in your car and drive to Beaver Brook Lodge and Restaurant near Evergreen." I called ahead to make sure someone was home. A friendly male voice told me to park in the rear and go to the back door.

It was an October day with the leaves in fall colors, golden aspens and dark red oaks. A misty rain was falling. The hills above Evergreen were lost in a drifting fog. As I drove nearer, my car climbing and twisting up the mountain road, an excitement I'd never felt before, came over me. I have a feeling, a premonition, I thought. I'm about to find the perfect cook. But, I warned myself, don't be too optimistic, Edna.

Beaver Brook Lodge was an old fashioned log building with a sweeping veranda commanding a view for miles over the meadows and hills.

Parking my car at the back, I walked up to a screen door and knocked. A short, jolly-looking fellow with white hair and goatee opened the door and invited me in. He looks like a retired sea captain, I thought as I entered the kitchen.

At a huge range stood a motherly-looking, white-haired lady. Since I had called ahead, she knew who I was. She led me into the dining room and seated me at a table next to a large window. "I'm Mrs. Mehlhorn and this is my husband Lloyd. Please call me 'Gert' as that's what I'm used to being called," she explained with a smile.

"One can see the lights of Denver in the distance on evenings when we have clear weather," her husband told me. They were the owner-managers of the lodge.

"This place is a lot like our Ski Tip," I exclaimed. "I feel right at home here. With no buildings to be seen anywhere, and with the rolling meadows, I feel like I'm back in pioneer days."

Gert started asking questions in a comfortable way. Soon, I realized that here was someone who knew more about, not only cooking, but running a lodge business, and handling the crew. She told me her husband had a job in Denver but would come up on Saturdays, "in time to carve the prime rib." Would I mind if she did the ordering? The menus she'd work out with me so that we could order enough to go right through to January.

"Great," I said. "But, how can we haul in so much? Where can we

174

store it all?''

"You tell me you are building a new wing with a much bigger kitchen. If the man who is doing the building is any good, he can build you a walk-in cooler, onto the kitchen.''

"Tell you what,'' Gert said. "I'll come up this weekend and tell him just what's needed. As far as hauling all the stuff up, didn't you know these wholesale meat and produce houses will haul it free to your door?''

Here, I'd been driving Loveland Pass through blizzards and God knows what, and buying at retail stores like Safeway!

"All you need to do,'' Gert said, "is give the wholesale companies your store license. You won't pay any tax, either.''

"Tax? Store license? I don't have any store license,'' I told Gert.

"You mean you've been in business all these years and haven't had a license? How on earth did you get away with it?'' Gert was astounded.

"We've been busy with other things, like skiing, mining, and ranching in the summer with horses for ourselves and friends. Nobody ever asked us about licenses.''

"Well, you can tell anyone who comes asking, that you are a dude ranch,'' Gert assured me. "Dude ranches don't have to have a license. At least they haven't needed any up till now.'' She also told me that if we ever wanted to put in a real bar, we'd have to have a license. She pointed out that with a store license and buying at wholesale, we would save enough not to mind the extra book work.

Max and the carpenter followed Gert's directions. We soon had two big freezers and a walk-in cooler. She redesigned our kitchen, creating a "no-man's-land'' area for herself. No guests would walk through and get in her way.

We worked out two-week menus to rotate. Any guest staying that long would be served something new each night, except on Saturday, which would always be prime rib night. The produce and hotel supply salesmen came. Then came the big trucks with everything we needed. In November came the bill, $1,400! I almost fainted. Seeing me begin to have qualms, Gert laughed and told me to relax. Except for the meat, fresh vegetables, and dairy supplies, the next order didn't go in until the first of March.

Bonnie was still with us and delighted with Gert. In the mornings she would rush down, sleepy-eyed, to set the breakfast table, but first, giving Gert a big hug. There would be no slapping on the cheek by this cook.

Things changed all around. Soon breakfast tables were set up the night before, after supper, "When the kids are awake enough to remember everything to put on the table," Gert would say.

Each morning I would have to post the number of guests, family and help. The first of each month, I had to list the approximate number of guests expected for each day of the month. The first of each week, I'd re-do this list.

Besides rules and lists posted in the kitchen, Gert would put up the day's menu. It didn't take long for the girls to stop asking, "Soup tonight, Gert?" She'd just say, "Look at the menu."

Besides correcting, making them behave, and being sympathetic, Gert had fun with the crew. If they decided to go to a movie in Breckenridge, they took her along. If it was over to Climax for some night skiing, she'd go along and watch with delight from the shelter window, bringing enough beer to quench everyone's thirst for the long ride home. She withheld the beer from the driver, but would hand whoever that was a coke.

Gert was a great knitter and a crocheter. She would ask the skiers to show her the latest styles. After dinner, she'd sit in the rathskeller, near the kitchen door, keeping an ear out for the soup simmering away for the next day. Guests would walk by and stop to admire the ski hat she'd be knitting. Not only Max and the crew appeared on the slopes wearing Gert's hats, but the guests too. That first winter she knitted and sold over 200 hats!

Spring came and skiing was over. Gert had to return to her Beaver Brook Lodge to be open by Mother's Day. She announced to me one day, "Edna, make out a list of all the canned goods you've got as leftovers. I'll buy them from you for our lodge. Come fall, I'll bring what I have left and you can buy that." It was the best arrangement I'd had.

Not only did my leftover canned goods follow Gert, but my entire crew did too! They helped her clean up her place, getting it ready to open. Some of them stayed on all summer to work for her. After all, she had trained them.

Gert was with us for five ski seasons, probably some of the happiest times at Ski Tip we remember.

One summer day a former guest came up to Ski Tip to just relax and visit. She was a newswriter for a Denver paper. Having written an article on Ski Tip the year before, I thought, how wonderful if she could do an item on Beaver Brook. I broached the idea to her. "Wonderful, I'll do it," she said. Little did I realize this was my undoing.

The article on Beaver Brook was two pages with pictures of Gert, the entire family and the menus, besides an excellent picture of the lodge. They were deluged with guests. Soon, it was *the place* to go. I was delighted, never dreaming I'd lost Gert.

Fall came, time for Gert to call about returning. She drove up one day to tell me they had sold the place. I knew they had listed it several times. They both felt, being in their sixties, it would soon be too much.

After all the publicity giving them a profitable summer, they were offered, and accepted, much more than they had dreamed of asking in the past. As Gert put it, "It just boils down to the fact, Edna, that you can't afford me any longer."

How true that was. She was priceless. For years I kept looking for another Gert. Finally, as one guest told me, "You'll just have to accept the fact, Edna. You'll never find another Gert."

As the years went by we graduated to two cooks, one a chef and one a breakfast cook. We also had a reservations clerk. Things became easier even though we had over 60 guests. However, I often thought back, a bit nostalgically, to those enjoyable haphazard times when 12 guests made a full house.

We were probably lucky that our ski-bums were usually the offspring of our guests. It wasn't unusual to have a parent call and ask if their daughter could work a winter season. "She's at college now, Edna, and just wants a year away, or maybe just a semester." Or, "She's so eager to become a really good skier. Her one or two week vacations aren't enough."

Quite soon I found we had the best source of well-behaved, fun-loving, get-along-with-the-guests, ski-bums possible. What was more, they really worked uncomplainingly. Perhaps entertaining was common at home, and they were required to help there too.

They enjoyed one thing we had not had before. That was to carry out a few of the college sorority or fraternity jokes at Ski Tip.

Coming home from skiing one day, I heard hilarious laughter down the hall. Our most dignified North Shore Chicago couple were standing at the door to their room and were convulsed with laughter. Jim, one of our ski-bums was standing to the side and saying, "Aha, we'd suspected you had smuggled a third guest into your room!" Jim and his two conspirators had taken a rubber Santa Claus mask, removed all the whiskers so only fat reddish cheeks showed, and had put a frowsy red wig on top. Stuffing a pair of pajamas with pillows, putting rubber gloves on the ends of the sleeves, and then tucking all this apparatus under the covers, it looked quite lifelike and comfortably over-fed. One rubber-gloved "hand" held a can of beer, the other the book *By Love Possessed*.

This started a, "You-put-one-over-on-me, I'll-get-back-at-you," chain reaction. I never knew what the guests would do in retaliation to Jim. One night at one a.m., four of them crept into the dorm room where Jim slept in one of the upper bunks. Taking hold of each corner of his mattress, they heaved, and out he came onto the floor, mattress and all.

Not satisfied with this, the ski-bums and the guests started writing limericks about each other. They started singing them on the slopes. For us not to feel left out, I'm sure, they wrote a song about Ski Tip. When Max and I entered the dining room for supper, they were well-rehearsed:

Oh it never snows in Arapahoe
Parlez-vous
It never snows in Arapahoe
Parlez-vous
Oh it never snows in Arapahoe
The drinking's fast but the skiing's slow
Rinky dinky parlez-vous

Oh we never eat at Ski Tip Lodge
Parlez-vous
We never eat at Ski Tip Lodge
Parlez-vous
We never eat but we drink our fill
And clobber down all over the hill
Rinky dinky parlez-vous

178

Oh Edna and Max run a Bum Hotel
  Parlez-vous
Oh Edna and Max run a Bum Hotel
  Parlez-vous
Oh Edna and Max run a Bum Hotel
But we love to ski so "What the hell!"
  Rinky dinky parlez-vous

But Hazel is a wonderful cook
  Parlez-vous
Yes Hazel is a wonderful cook
  Parlez-vous
Oh Hazel is a wonderful cook
She dishes up such amazing gook
  Rinky dinky parlez-vous

Oh Little Dorey and Baby Alice
  are helpful too
Yes Little Dorey and Baby Alice
  are helpful too
Yes Alice and Dorey are helpful too
They stir the gook and serve the goo
  Rinky dinky parlez-vous

Oh it never snows at Arapahoe, etc.

I believe the guests rejuvenated all the "hanky-panky" each season. With each new crew, away it went again. The ski-bums joyfully would retaliate. A guest would come back from skiing to find his p.j.s on top of his well-made bed, or hung on the door, only they had been washed, starched, and then ironed. Years later he would continue to tell the story of how he still couldn't get into them. Or have a guest announce he would like the cook to bake a cake as one of the party was having a birthday. The lovely cake would appear all lighted with candles. One of the ski-bums would carry it in with the entire crew following. Everyone would join in singing, "Happy Birthday."

The honored guest would blow out the candles, pleased at all this attention, and begin to cut the cake. He would cut and saw away, unaware that the cake was a cardboard shoe box covered with mint-colored shaving cream. I was always apprehensive as to how the guests would accept these jokes. They loved them and were rewarded with a real cake right afterwards. It got to the point where guests felt ignored if they didn't have **179** this kind of trick played on them.

On the cook's night off, with more restaurants in the area, we encouraged the guests to eat out. I had, happily, gotten out of the habit of cooking.

We had one guest, Vern, a favorite of all at Ski Tip, who loved the pranks and enjoyed finding ways to retaliate. This one night, cook's night out, we had thought up a new way to fool him. The crew told him they were eating out, and he was invited to join them. He accepted with pleasure.

We had reserved a table at a new Italian restaurant near Frisco. Calling ahead to the proprietors, I requested that we be served a spaghetti dinner. Only one plate served would be different. It would have white wool yarn with meat balls and spaghetti sauce heaped on top. Purchasing the yarn that afternoon, I brought it in to the restaurant ahead of time. They were aghast, but complied. I told them I would point out to them the guest who was to be served this dish.

We were shown to a table and Vern sat down with a happy sigh between our two pretty Italian-Swiss ski-bums. They started in with gusto, twisting their spaghetti with spoon and fork. He looked at them scornfully, "I eat my spaghetti the American way."

He struggled with fork and knife, becoming a little frustrated, then a bit puzzled. Finally, he looked closely at the spaghetti. Then leaning back he exclaimed, "I didn't think you kids could get away with anything *away* from Ski Tip." He loved it. Years later we heard him telling other guests about that dinner.

Most of our ski-bums came from families who could have picked up our mortgage as easily as buying a new pair of Head skis. This was a comfortable feeling for us. There was never any worry about their quitting because they wanted more pay. In the early years at Ski Tip, they often worked for no more than room, board, and tips. Sometimes, when they asked to work a season or a semester from school, they even offered to pay us.

Then again, with their affluent upbringing, they couldn't understand why I objected to their filling the glasses to the brim with milk the second or third time. They did it even when the guests hadn't asked for more.

*Our swinging guest,
a ski-bum special.*

*Delighted guest
shows Oma, Sunni
and husband Alf,
recipes from our
wonderful cook,
Gert, left.*

*A guest teaches me
how to build a
Black Russian.*

181

Berit, our Norwegian ski-bum teaches the schottische.

Hazel (left), "Baby Alice" and "Little Dorey" too, cook the gook and serve up the goo.

Departing guests receive a dancing send-off by our cook and crew.

182

I usually got back from ski school around four p.m. One day I came home to find the cook frantically unloading the shelves in the cooler. "Edna, you've got ham on the menu and there positively is none. I've searched everywhere."

"I'll help you look," I told her, thinking that she probably looked right at it and hadn't seen it. We searched to no avail. Fortunately, we were able to substitute something else. I was really puzzled as I knew I'd bought the ham and had unloaded it.

All came to light the next morning. Arriving at ski school, I was told the cook over at the Basin shelter wanted to see me. Whatever for? I wondered. "Edna," she blasted at me as I came in the door, "it's hard enough for me to make money on the lunches in the middle of the week, without having one of your ski-bums sitting out there in the sun on the porch, making ham sandwiches for all her friends, plus anyone else who wants to join in."

Came the light. "Aha," I said, "now I know what happened to that ham we were to have last night. I wonder if there's any bread, lettuce, mayonnaise or mustard left." Assuring the cook up at the Arapahoe shelter that it wouldn't happen again, I wondered how best to explain to our generous ski-bum that Ski Tip couldn't afford to feed the skiers up at Arapahoe.

Sometimes the ski-bums would take over the entertainment of the guests in a most surprising way. One young girl loved dressing up so no one would recognize her. She would appear as another guest, arriving at the front door, luggage and all. She would then act out the role of a most obnoxious guest. Most everyone would soon catch on and enjoy the act.

One time, however, our ski-bum actress left our guests not too sure. The door from the kitchen into the living room was thrown open and in walked a stocky figure, carrying a toilet plunger and wearing a hard hat, and rubber boots. I stood up, wondering who this mustachioed person was. Just as I was about to ask him, he stated, "I'm the plumber." He looked around long enough to be sure he'd captured everyone's attention, and announced, "Don't anyone flush a toilet for three days." Someone started to laugh. Suddenly, as the plumber laughed, we all knew who she was.

We felt we had really arrived when Willy Schaeffler brought Stein Erickson, the famous Norwegian Olympic racer, to Ski Tip. He was at the area for the ski instructors' meeting. Since all the examiners stayed at Ski Tip, the parties were held there in the evenings. What fun we had! Everyone who could play a guitar or accordian brought an instrument along. With Swiss yodeling, Bavarian and Italian songs, the music went on sometimes into the late hours. Max loved it and joined in with his clarinet. The evening Stein was there, I suggested Max play some of the Norwegian songs he'd learned, such as *Paul Paa Haugen,* or *Per Spellemand.* It was a great hit.

The year following, when Bonnie was at Ski Tip, we were hoping Stein might return. One day, before supper, Bonnie called to me. "Guess what, Edna? Someone calling himself Stein Erickson phoned today. He asked to reserve a room during the ski instructors' meeting."

"Well?" I asked, "What did you tell him?"

"Tell him?" she answered. "When he said the second time he was Stein Erickson, I said, 'You're kidding!' and hung up."

After reaching Stein in Aspen and apologizing for Bonnie's compliment-in-reverse, he just laughed, assuring me he'd be over for some more Norwegian singing.

It was much easier for the guests to wait on themselves when it came to buying postcards or stamps. We kept the stamps in a wooden cup on the shelf in the dining room plus assorted cards. With change left in the cup, they could buy stamps and cards, putting the money in the cup, making their own change.

My cook took me aside one day and confided, "I think you better talk to Bonnie. She loves Coca-Cola, as you know, but she takes a dime out of the stamp cup and buys her coke with it. This was in the days when you got a large coke out of our pop machine for a dime. We had to buy the machine and it was supposed to pay for itself with the dimes put in. By the time it was paid for, the cokes were costing us fifteen cents. The guests had to pay only a dime.

I knew Bonnie was honest and asked her. "But, Edna, you get the

184

dime back when you empty the coin box!"

The guests loved Bonnie. I soon realized it would be easier on me if Bonnie would collect their bills which I'd made out the night before they checked out. One morning, as she was rushing around making beds, I saw a twenty dollar bill sticking out of her moccasin. On my pointing it out to her, she took her moccasin off. Inside was all the money and checks which she had collected that morning. "I haven't had time to run down to the basement yet," she explained, "to put it all in the safe behind the furnace." We were never a penny short.

"I guess those moccasins are as safe as anything else around here," I laughed as I took off for ski school.

"Why don't you and Max advertise as a bloody matrimonial bureau," one guest remarked to us. "You'd certainly do a lot better, profit-wise, that is," he added.

We had just arrived at his home in Chicago to attend the wedding of one of our ski-bums from the winter past. She was marrying one of the ski instructors. It was fun, going to all those weddings.

I had second thoughts one fall when a parent called us. "Our second daughter wants to come out and ski-bum for a winter." He added, "if this one gets married too, it'll be the end of a long friendship." Fortunately, the second daughter's marriage was also a happy one. We are still good friends. If today we were hosts at Ski Tip, we would be skiing with their grandchildren.

Larry Jump brought Bernie Pomagalski down to Ski Tip one day early in the season. Bernie, a 19-year-old French boy, could not speak more than a half dozen words in English. We needed a dishwasher and Bernie was willing to be one for room and board. During the day, he would help out at the ski area. His father, Jean Pomagalski, had sold a Poma ski lift to Arapahoe.

Bernie was a charming young bull-in-a-china-shop. The daily crash from the kitchen and the guests would smile, "Bernie broke another dish!" When they teased him about it, he would say, "I don't deeg you." The kitchen crew was fast teaching him their brand of English.

185

Bernie had been on the French National Junior Ski Team. He was one of the first skiers we had seen who could *wedel* down the slopes in beautiful style.

One evening a guest came running into the living room from the hall of the old wing. "There's a bear standing near our window!"

We all rushed to the room. Looking out of the window we saw a young black bear standing next to a pine tree. He looked as frightened as we.

"I catch zees bear!" Bernie came running around the corner from the kitchen. "I catch zees cute bear!"

"Don't you dare go near that bear! Get back in the kitchen." I was glad the window was open or he would not have heard me. Seeing cheeses on the outside of the window sill to keep cool for the usual room party, I realized what had attracted the bear.

Wanting to make sure Bernie obeyed me, I returned to the kitchen. There was much commotion at the outside door. Bernie had put on a big parka with fur hood, leather mittens and ski goggles. "Now, I catch zees bear," he announced.

I caught the tail end of the parka. Petunia came to help and we pulled Bernie back into the kitchen. "It's an order, Bernie." I emphatically stated, "Absolutely No! No catch zees bear." Looking over to the pine tree I saw the frightened bear climbing the tree as fast as he could. We were all safe.

For several years in the spring, George and Patti Nelson would come down from their Lutsen Resort in Minnesota to stay at Ski Tip and attend the annual ski instructors clinic. Both became certified ski instructors. No wonder that their daughter, Cindy, became a member of the U.S. Olympic team.

The spring Bernie was with us, the Nelsons invited him to come up and work at their resort on Lake Superior.

Returning in the fall, Bernie related to us his beautiful summer at Lutsen. "Only one thing I was not happy with," he told us. "I could not have a whole pie like Petunia let me have here. Pet, she always bake me a whole pie—just for me!"

Had I known, he would not have had a whole pie at Ski Tip either!

14

"Bend Zee Knees."

Why I wanted to become a ski instructor, I had no idea. Perhaps it was because I felt I had something to impart that would help beginners. After teaching the school kids on the hill behind the old baseball field in Breckenridge, I must have felt I'd had some experience. During four years at the Court House I had been able to persuade my deputy to stay in the office after four p.m. on Tuesdays and Thursdays. I would meet the school kids at the field and teach them as best I could. In return for this sacrifice on my deputy's part, I did the same for her in the summer months.

Ski instructors seemed to have so much fun. Perhaps that was my main reason, to be a part of that elite group of which Max was a member.

My first and futile attempt at taking the ski instructor's certification examination was back in '48. This exam was a one-day affair held at Berthoud Pass.

We were told to meet the first examiner who would put us through the beginning stage at the top of the hill. This was the steepest part of the area. There we would demonstrate the snowplow and the beginning part of teaching. I remember the examiner was Rudi Schnackenberg. I made the comment, "I doubt I'd want to take a beginning skier up here." Rudi said nothing but I felt from his expression that he heartily agreed with me. Later, I found out that each examiner was told where to stand.

As I progressed down the hill to each "station" the stage of teaching became more advanced, until I was at the almost flat bottom of the hill where we were to demonstrate the parallel turn. I wondered if I would have enough momentum to accomplish two turns, so did only one.

The examiner looked at me and said, "I've never heard of you. Besides, you're supposed to do two turns, like this." He proceeded to demonstrate. On his second turn, he overturned and skidded backwards into a wind-formed hollow beneath a large spruce tree.

After helping him out of the hole, I asked him, "Like that, you mean? And, come to think of it, I've never heard of you, either!" I was not surprised at the end of the day when I was informed that I hadn't passed.

Willy Schaeffler came to Arapahoe that fall. How the ski instructor's examination changed! What a contrast to the previous year's forest ranger, teen-age ski racer, and president of the Rocky Mountain Ski Association "examiner" types. Some of them had never taught a day of skiing! The exception was Rudi who was very well qualified to teach and examine.

Willy's arrangements included only examiners who were ski instructors of long standing: Ernie Blake, ski school director of Santa Fe Ski Basin, and later Taos Ski Valley; George Engle, director of the Winter Park Ski School; plus of course Rudi and Max, who seemed happy to be with people who knew what they were doing.

Examination day arrived after several grueling days of skiing with these men. For the final test I would go through teaching all of the turns having each one of the men as the pupil and I as teacher. Just as I was getting into the lift line to go up the mountain to meet the examiners, way up in Lenawee Park, the chair lift broke down. We were told it would be down the rest of the day. What to do? The only choice was to climb.

I climbed and climbed until I thought I would collapse. I made it to the exam point just in time. Thankfully, they were sympathetic and let me catch my breath enough so I could begin to teach. Most important was to correct their obvious and deliberate mistakes. In the evenings we had written tests. At the end of that evening's exam, I was told I had passed. I felt jubilant because I knew I had passed a good hard, and complete test, not a slipshod one.

That evening I couldn't help but think back to that test, four years before, when I had awaited my turn at a station. While there I had overheard a man say as he came up to one of the examiners, "You've gotta pass Miss So&So. She's gonna be teaching at a girl's school in Denver."

It was a thrill for me to be a certified instructor for I couldn't think of anything more rewarding than bringing a beginner from an awkward, tense snowplow to a relaxed and more graceful parallel turn.

It wasn't much longer before we began the ski season with the large Rocky Mountain News-Willy Schaeffler Ski School. Almost all of the classes consisted of complete beginners. The practice slope was like a human ant hill with the classes practically back to back. There was, however, an excellent open bowl at Midway. It had the best runout to slow down the beginners. The problem for the instructor was how to get the morning class down after the first lesson, and still be ready for the afternoon class starting at one o'clock.

I hit on a wonderful idea. One of our pretty ski-bums, who could ski quite well, wanted to become a ski instructor. I told her to hurry through her work in the morning, drive up to the Basin, go right up to Midway where she could arrive just as I started my class down the road. It worked beautifully. The class had learned to snowplow, snowplow turn, and step turn around. Skiing down this easy road gave the beginners the feeling of constant movement forward without having to climb back up and wait their turn. With the ski-bum bringing up the rear, she could check on anyone lagging behind or help novices get up after a fall. This eliminated my having to climb back up to help. Then the rest of the class was not kept waiting. Soon, with many eager, wishing-to-be-instructors, the ski school had enough help to give each instructor an apprentice.

Apprentices were of great help as the classes grew. I can remember having a class of 28 one Saturday. It was hard to keep track of who was in the class and who was just skiing past. Many a surprised skier would look up at me wondering why I was yelling my comments at him.

I had believed that being a ski instructor would help me become a much better racer. How wrong I was! After days of teaching beginners and intermediates, I found I had been exaggerating or over-demonstrating a turn. At that time we were teaching the old Arlberg technique which didn't help my slalom one bit.

One instructor-supervisor advised me to tell my class that the best way to get a good swing of the downhill arm forward on a "rotation" turn, was to pretend you were taking a handkerchief out of your back pocket and reach forward with it as if you were trying to give it to some-one. That was hard for me to do. I didn't even have a back pocket. I was glad when Max advised me to disregard that bit of advice because in slalom, I found I was beginning to rotate my upper body in the gate.

When Erich Windisch arrived from Garmish to teach at Arapahoe, he brought with him the new Austrian technique. He showed me my

190

mistakes in slalom and gave me more advanced classes now and then. Also, he arranged for me to teach a group of young women from Loretto Heights College who wanted to form a racing club. I shall never forget one of them saying to me, "It's a great help to see you running gates. We all tell ourselves, 'If she can do it, we can.'"

"If I can do it, you can." I borrowed this phrase when teaching regular classes, knowing most members of the classes were considerably younger than I. It always made them laugh and relax.

When pupils progressed they would often show their delight by writing embellished accounts of what excellent skiers they'd become. Their letters to the ski school would praise their instructor as the very best. Since all of us received this kind of elaborate praise, we realized it really didn't matter who they had for an instructor. We all taught, and had to teach, pretty much alike.

It was fun when the pupils' appreciation went as far as bringing presents. One grateful fellow brought me armfuls of aluminum foil in all shapes; freezer wrap, pie tins, waste baskets, and other items. These gifts were most needed at Ski Tip. He was a salesman for an aluminum company, of course.

Sometimes in those early years, being the only woman ski instructor in the school could be amusingly embarrassing. One late afternoon when the supervisors were critiquing our performance of the day, one of them said, "It's O.K. to give attention to a pretty female of receptive temperament, but don't give her all of your attention excluding the others in the class. Be nice to her, but you know, you don't have to sleep with her." Seeing me over in the corner, he added, "Sorry, Edna, I didn't mean you."

I laughed, "That's all right. Just as long as you include Max!"

In May of 1961 Max and I thought we would like to take a vacation and at the same time attend the annual meeting of the Technical Coordinating Committee of the National Ski Association. This was to be held at Big Mountain Ski Area in Montana. I looked forward to being a late riser and maybe go skiing if I felt like it. In other words, I could be the type of guest we didn't tolerate very often at Ski Tip.

The first morning Max woke me at five a.m. "We have to be up on the mountain early this morning."

"Why on earth *so* early?" I wondered aloud.

After breakfast we headed up the mountain. Congregated at the top were many of the most famous ski instructors and directors of ski schools I'd ever heard of. They were from all over the U.S. Sun Valley was represented by Sigi Engl; from New Hampshire came Herbert Schneider, son of the famous Hannes Schneider who was the father of the Arlberg technique; Curt Chase of Red Lodge, Montana, later director of Aspen Ski School; and Doug Pfeiffer of California, a writer for *SKIING* and *SKI* magazines. Also we saw Bill Lash, Jim Johnston, Paul Valar, and Don Rhinehart. There was a sense of excitement in the air.

They didn't seem to be interested in skiing down the mountain. Instead, they stood around in groups, discussing ski techniques. Once in a while someone would demonstrate the point he was trying to make. Wanting a vacation away from ski school, I skied off by myself. The trees were still covered by heavy snow, making them look like funny gnomes and the view off to the south toward the blue waters of immense Flathead Lake was magnificent. To the east I could see the peaks of Glacier National Park.

Thinking I'd retire early that evening, after all we'd gotten up at *five a.m.,* I was grateful when Max told me to go ahead. "Get a good night's sleep. I'll come in later, maybe quite late. I have a meeting." He was up again at five a.m. the next morning, but thoughtfully didn't awaken me.

Attending the afternoon meeting of the ski instructors, I realized something significant was occurring. Out of this five-day meeting, an organization called the "Professional Ski Instructors of America, Inc.," would become official. The American Ski Technique agreed upon there would become in a few years the accepted teaching method in the majority of the ski schools in the entire United States. It has evolved today into ATM, the American Teaching Method.

The Arlberg technique was what I first taught. I had heard of, but not seen, the French technique, the Emile Allais style of teaching. In the fall of 1957, Willy Schaeffler introduced the Austrian technique to the ski school

192

"That's it! Now you're really sliding," I tell a youngster on her first day.

"Oh, God!" They're watching me!" Three critical examiners scrutinizing each hopeful would-be ski instructor: George Engle, Max Dercum and Willy Schaeffler.

193

at Arapahoe. Max had assisted the year before in translating from the official Austrian Ski Technique book. At that time, by Willy's suggestion, Max had begun teaching this to a few selected pupils. There were mixed emotions in the ski school among a few of the instructors, but with the arrival of Erich Windisch to help clinic all of us in this new way of skiing and teaching, everyone accepted it. Everyone, I should say, except one. He left to join another school leaving us a compatible group.

There was, at first, controversy throughout the ski-teaching world. The word *wedeln* became familiar to skiers. I remember reading somewhere the comment of quick-witted Fred Iselin, who was co-director with Friedl Pfeiffer of the Aspen Ski School. "We teach Friedlin and Fredelin over here." Others would ask us, "How does it feel to stand crooked on the hill?" The body was angulated, with upper body facing downhill and since this was different from the Arlberg stance in a traverse, it often was derided. A few instructors, at some of the other schools, wanted to teach this new technique. They told us later, "We had to teach behind the bushes," so to speak.

This variety of techniques really confused ski pupils. They might take a lesson at Arapahoe, then go to Aspen, where a modified Arlberg technique was taught, then to Stein Erickson's Norwegian ski school over at the Highlands, and then lessons at Sun Valley with a French ski instructor. Something had to be done.

The formation of a universal ski-teaching technique was necessary, at least in the U.S.

It was fun listening to all the arguments, the pros and cons, at Big Mountain. I was so proud of Max, when at the end of it all, the nucleus of the PSIA (Professional Ski Instructors of America) was formed. He was one of the seven founders along with Curt Chase, Bill Lash, Doug Pfeiffer, Jim Johnston, Don Rhinehart and Paul Valar.

For years I was madly rushing Ski Tip guests through the breakfasts I'd cooked for them so I could be up at Arapahoe in time for the first class of the morning. Meanwhile Max was giving free ski lessons at the breakfast table with our huskies, Kiska and Taku, peering through the window. Standing in front of my class I was very much out of breath from

194

all the rush, limp from the heat of the kitchen stove, and wondering if I still smelled of frying bacon.

When we acquired more help, plus a breakfast cook, it became less hectic to reach the area and my class. As I grew older it became harder for me to lift up the overweight beginners who couldn't get up after falling down. I began to question the benefit of it all.

My decision to give up teaching came to me clearly one afternoon after I had been handling beginners all day at the bottom of the practice slope at Arapahoe Basin. The cheery voice of a friend carried through the air to me as she skied by, "Oh, Edna, you should see the Pali! The snow is fantastic and the skiing is sublime."

It was a beautiful Christmas holiday, 18 years after I'd started teaching at Arapahoe. I quit that day.

195

15

Over the Hill Vets Racing

Willy Schaeffler decided this racing against a bunch of "youngsters" wasn't for us. A new kind of race would be inaugurated—the National Vets Giant Slalom. Also we were to have the Masters Race which would be for ski instructors only.

To quote from the *American Ski Annual,* "The first running on April 26th, 1953, of the National Senior Giant Slalom championships will be held on the Palivacini at Arapahoe Basin."

There were only seven women of us so we all raced in the same age group, 32 and over. It was thought no woman would admit to being any older. Jean Litchfield, the winner, was presented a special medal for admitting to being the oldest.

From the local Summit County Journal: "Climaxing a gala weekend, a banquet was held at the Dillon school, with Helen Rich, well-known Breckenridge author as guest of honor. She described the skiing feats of Father Dyer, who back in the 1880's skied over the mountain passes from Fairplay on his 12-foot skis to preach in the mining camps." To our skeptical ears she quoted him as telling how he went so fast sometimes that his skis caught on fire. "Now I know," I told Helen, "where the phrase comes from, 'Burning up the slopes with my skis.'"

A new exciting type of racing for older skiers had begun. Just previously there had been an alpine race back east for 32-year-olds and over, but we felt ours was the first truly national one since racers came from California, Arizona, and back east, Karl Acker from Pico Peak, and others, whereas at Franconia the racers were all from nearby.

Perhaps the greatest time many of us ever had at a Veterans race after that was at Santa Fe, New Mexico. This was in March of 1955. Having never been to that state I was eager to see it. I had heard of the Pueblo Indians and the Navajos. Seppi Olmi, our good friend, artist, guitarist, and Winter Park ski instructor had told us of the area and of the Spanish and Indian influences down there. It all sounded so colorful. I regretted that Max could not come too. Max had not been racing because he was busy keeping the ski school running seven days a week. Besides, Willy was the best racer to uphold our division.

Off to Santa Fe we went, leaving Dillon at three a.m. I almost grabbed the wrong skis in the dark. John Bailey drove, while Seppi, his son Toni, and I and George Engle of Winter Park were the passengers. We were to meet Dottie and Rudi Schnackenberg down there. We had been invited to stay at the home of a friend of Seppi's.

Stopping for breakfast near Poncha Springs at a small cafe, we found a toy for sale at the counter. It was just a small, round box, but when turned over it "mooed" loudly just like a cow right at your elbow. "We've got to have this." I can't remember who bought it or said, "I'll turn it over just as Willy is ready to push out of the starting gate."

We arrived at a lovely Spanish home surrounded by big cotton-woods and with beautiful verandas. Our hostess, wearing white coveralls with RAF on the front, greeted us, "Oh, you'll have to excuse my appearance. I've been up in the tree with Jesus all morning and I'm getting a divorce at two." I thought, is she some kind of a religious nut? I'll have to ask Seppi what that was all about. I was very tired from the long drive but delighted to find myself in a lovely room with my own veranda and the trees leafing out already although it was still snow season at home. I soon forgot about my Jesus question and changed to ski clothes. We had to get up the 25 miles to the ski area before noon. Ernie Blake, who then managed the area, had told us that all traffic went up till noon. After that it was all downhill traffic as the road was too narrow for two cars to pass.

So, off we went to the Santa Fe Ski Basin.

The sun was very warm and the snow was very wet. The chairlift had broken down ten minutes before we arrived. So, we began climbing from the bottom. Willy was there. Grant Ford, president of the Rocky Mountain Division prepared to set the course. All the men stripped to the waist but the women climbed and perspired. Hope the men all get sunburned, I wished. They're the lucky ones. Never have to wait till they get to the bottom to go to the bathroom, just wander off into the woods. The next time anyone asks me what I'm thinking while standing in the starting gate, I'll tell them. It's a funny thing, I thought as I continued to climb, after I get through the finish gate I don't have to go anymore.

A cool wind started to blow as we got higher up. To the west we could see a reddish-looking haze. "We're in for a dust storm," someone said. I wondered what it would be like skiing in a dust storm.

Reaching the top we rested a bit and then started to look at the slalom. Rocks, grass, ice, and a narrow gully between gates for the first 300 feet! Rudi advised me, "Use the old Winter Park snowplow." We found one gate with a big hole in the middle with a huge rock protruding out of it. To prevent further trouble, we took up the rest of the gates and blocked the entire trail. Grant had decided to reset the whole course. The men carried shovels up to help him and the rest of us climbed back up to the start which was to be 300 feet below the original one. I knew Grant had not set that one. It was getting dark with the dust beginning to blow. The wet snow gradually turned to brown-colored ice.

Back down to Santa Fe and the La Fonda Hotel where we were to be guests at a cocktail party. Someone asked me if I'd like a beefeater. "Oh, I'd love one," I answered, thinking, "I don't care what kind of a steak it is, I'm so hungry." Thanking whoever handed me a martini, I wondered when they would serve the beefeater steak. Big bowls of dip were brought in, avocado and other kinds new to me. But there were no crackers or anything else, just the dip decorated with bib lettuce around the sides. What to do? Someone, hungrier than I, tore off a piece of the lettuce and scooped up some of the dip. We all followed suit and when the lettuce was all gone we just "stuck in our thumbs and pulled out. . ." more dip. The drinks were great and so was the mariachi music. But having been up since three a.m., we were most grateful when we were

198

whisked to another beautiful adobe home and a big buffet dinner. Racing with the "young 'uns" was never like this, I thought, as I filled my plate with delicious food and someone handed me another drink.

I cornered Seppi. "By the way, Seppi, is our hostess terribly religious? What did she mean when she said she'd been up in the tree with Jesus all morning?"

Seppi laughed. "Edna, here in New Mexico we have a lot of Spanish Americans and many of the boys are named Jesus. She was up in the tree with this boy she had hired to help her with the tree pruning."

Finally we got back to "our lovely adobe" and I fell into bed dead tired.

The morning of the race dawned with a blue, blue sky, not a cloud. This will be a great day, I told myself as I started to get out of bed. But, something, I swear, hit me on the back of my head as I started to get up. Oh, my head, I groaned. It was a struggle to get dressed and another struggle to get to the kitchen. I can't eat a thing, I beefed. Everyone was having strong, black coffee but I didn't even want that.

Ed Pelke, one of the racers staying there, was standing near the stove in bright green pajamas with big black polkadots. And he was drinking wine. "Here, have a slug of this dry wine." He offered me some from a jug hooked over his thumb.

"This is a nightmare, your pajamas," I answered, "and now I should drink wine?"

Each one insisted I drink something. "You've got to be in shape to win that race." I had some gingerale, then some aspirin and finally some coffee. What a way to train for a race! I bet all the others went to bed early.

Getting to the area we found the snow was solid ice with enough sand in it to polish my new Head skis till they shone like silver. Willy sharpened my edges so they would really hold on the icy course, and we all started up. Luckily the lift was working, but from the top of the lift we had to ski over to a queer looking rope tow which could only take four skiers at a time. It was short and we had to straddle the rocks almost doing the splits to miss them.

199   We had to take off our skis to climb what was known as the "burn."

With the wind blowing hard and cold, my neck began to feel stiff from carrying the skis. Finally we got to the top and to the start. The climb and the cold air had helped clear my head. Also the fact that my friends were behind me cracking the whip. "Keep going," had been the chant.

Ed Pelke was already there with his thumb still curled around his wine jug. Years later I asked someone if they'd seen Ed. "Not since he went through the starting gate at the Santa Fe race holding on to that jug."

"Don't remember his going through the finish gate," someone else said, "and come to think of it, I don't think anyone's seen him since."

To this day, I'm sure, Willy feels that he'd have won that race and not come in second if he hadn't been startled by a noise. He had just started to pole out of the starting gate when a loud *moo* sounded right behind him. He checked, looked back, and then raced on. If anyone ever deserved a rerun, it was Willy that day.

How I ever made it down that course and won, I'll never know! No one cared to ski after the race so we all went down to Santa Fe and to Ernie and Rhoda Blake's lovely home for relaxing and some cold beer. Then to the La Fonda and a banquet and more mariachi music and the award ceremony. And, once in a while, we'd hear the moo cow in the background.

On the way back home the next morning I thought, if senior racing is like this, I'll have some—and more.

The wildest race for us was probably the Old Timers Olympics thought up by Ernie Blake who now owned and operated the famous and beautiful Taos Ski Area. This was in the end of March 1970 and we had just finished competing in the National Vets races at Vail. Vail had been most satisfying for us since Max was now racing with me, as also were our son Rolf and his wife, Judy. Both Rolf and Judy had reached the ripe old ages of 26 and 27 which qualified them as "Veterans." The age classification had dropped to 25 and over, and we were now separated into age groups: Class I, 25 to 32; Class II, 32 to 40; and so on. I was glad because at age 56 I had no desire to race against the 32-year-old-and-up classes.

Colonel Ed Link, energetic manager of the Crystal Mountain, Washington, ski area, had been racing at Vail. Being over 50 he decided

200

Santa Fe, New Mexico —Vet's National Giant Slalom, 1955

Over 50 Senior Olympics, Taos & Sandia Peak, New Mexico, 1970. (Edna wins Taos cup)

First Place winners —1970 National Vet's Race at Vail, Colo. All Dercums. Rolf, Max, Edna and Judy (Rolf's wife).

201

Crystal Mountain, Washington—1976 Jane Hough and Edna

NASTAR pacesetter, Max, 1972

St. Gervais, France 1981, Max wins his class in World Cup.

Sansicario, Italy, 1980, Edna wins her class in World Cup, No. 11 with No. 7, Georgene Bihlman, Calif., over-all winner.

202

to join us at Taos. What none of us realized, was that Sandia Peak ski area out of Albuquerque was also to host a couple of races. Arriving at Taos the night before the Taos giant slalom, Ernie Blake invited the three of us to an unforgettable dinner in Jean Mayer's Inn, the St. Bernard. Rare roast beef, and beautifully fragrant French wine were served in a truly French-Swiss atmosphere.

Why do I bother ski racing? I thought. Why don't I just become a "racer-chaser," and follow Max around, eat like this, laze in the warm sun and forget about the starting gate and all the gates thereafter. But, I knew the next morning I would only have to look at the start and I'd feel like an eager old race horse.

First day was the giant slalom, and the next day the slalom. At the end of that race, before eating, we had to drive madly down to Albuquerque. There we would be guests for cocktails at a lovely hacienda, then to the Old Town for dinner, and then to bed in a motel.

The next morning we took the tram up from the base of Sandia Peak. This carried us high above the mountainside but we could look down on warm jagged rocks with cactus about to bloom. Here and there we could see the mountain sheep lying down next to a rock or standing on a sharp pinnacle. I doubted we could ski once we got to the top as there was no snow in sight. This was desert country and I wondered if someone was playing a joke on us. But, after unloading in the big tramway house and stepping outside, we looked to the east and down a snowy slope, with well-groomed trails and a double chairlift already carrying early morning skiers up from the east side. From the restaurant, where we were given our race numbers, we could look in both directions to views too dramatic to describe.

We had a giant slalom to run. One of the racers, Ken Bartholemew, I noticed, had no ski poles. Riding up the chairlift with him I asked him why.

"Oh," he answered me, "you see, I've never raced in skiing before. In 1948 I won a gold medal in the Olympics in speed skating. When I heard of the ski race for over 50-year-olds, I thought I'd try it. I live in Minnesota and do some skiing. Thought it would be fun." I was going up the chairlift after my run when I saw him come down. He's doing what I did in my first race in '38, I thought.

Before our second run I asked Ken if he'd mind if I gave him a bit of advice.

"Glad for any," he said.

So I told him to turn before he got to the gate and not after he'd gone through the gate. I also added to my advice, "Use ski poles. You'll be able to push out of the start so much faster and then skate like hell, like you're in a speed skating race, but do turn before you get to the gate. At the bottom skate and pole to the finish gate." He did it all and came in third. Evidently once a competitor, always a competitor. The next March of '71, there he was up at Sun Valley with the rest of us for the Vets Nationals.

Back to Taos for the next day's race, a slalom, and then return to Albuquerque for the last race, another slalom and a awards banquet. It was all crazy, but we loved it. There was only one racer who wasn't sure. He was a former Polish Olympic racer, now living in New York, who had never realized the distances out in the west and that we thought nothing of it. He was the only hitchhiking racer but once he and his wife arranged rides with us, he seemed, even though in a confused state of mind, to enjoy it. Maybe that's why we didn't see him the next year at Sun Valley, or for that matter anywhere else out west.

It's been over 44 years of racing, many races funny, many thrilling, and some frustrating, such as the Eve Perkins Memorial Race at Berthoud Pass. On March 10, 1956, the *Southern Rocky Mountain Ski Notes* published the Class A results:

Mary Lind	1:06.8	1st
Beverly Paulich	1:09.4	2nd
Edna Dercum	1:01.7	3rd

I was listed as third and should have had first place. I was too timid at the end of the race to protest, even though our good friend, Hans Bookstrom, who had seen the results, told me to.

Having learned my lesson, I spoke up when it happened again. Two weeks after the 1956 May Day Race at Arapahoe, which I knew I had won, I received a letter and a gold pin from the race officials. "The humiliating aspect of the affair was that you did not receive the pin that you earned at the presentation of awards. Thanks for calling our attention to the questionable validity of the results.''

My biggest frustration, however, was at the Loveland Grand Prix in 1964. The race was a long and difficult giant slalom. Tensely and determined I tucked and schussed the last steep face. I knew I had raced well.

Running up to me after I had crossed the finish line one of the timers yelled, ''We didn't get your time. You will have to go back up and run again.'' I was exhausted, but down to the lift line I skied, then up the lift to the start where the men's races had already begun.

At the end of my rerun the timer came up to me. ''We didn't believe your first time because it was so good, so asked you to run again. You've won the race. We'll give you your first time as both times were very close." It made me furious to have been treated that way. Being older than most of the others was not always an advantage. No one believed this "50-year-old lady's time."

Since 1953 it has been Squaw Valley, Park City, Aspen, Sun Valley, Bogus Basin, Big Sky, Stevens Pass, Crystal Mountain, Copper Mountain and our first international racing in 1980 in Sansicario in Italy and Villars in Switzerland. The last two were for ages 40 and older, the *"Super-40 World Cup"* in Italy and the *"Coup de Monde des Anciennes Gloires"* in Switzerland. I'm sure this last must translate as, "ancients in their glory," for that's how we all felt.

At the race in Italy, my first international race, while standing in the starting gate with the usual nervous anticipation, I found I couldn't understand the starter. How will I know what he is saying when he counts me out of the gate? I was frantic, but upon hearing the word *uno* I shot out of the gate.

There wasn't that much difference in the 180 Veteran racers from over half a dozen countries in Europe than in those from the U.S. They had the same friendly congenial attitude. However, we noticed their life style of apparent wealth and they had the finest of equipment.

Winning the Veterans World Cups and gold medals in our age class were proud moments for Max and for me. I never dreamed we would be World Cup winners. This was the first year Americans had participated in these European races. Actually I won the combined medal for highest score in my class for the eight races. In the slalom at Villars, I was sixth over all women—40 and over. Max, who had stiffer competition, won the combined for four races. What satisfaction at ages 65 and 67!

In Italy, at the Over-40 World Cup, February, 1980, after checking the list of women racers I discovered, just like at races at home, I was the oldest woman racer there. Suddenly it dawned on me, I'm the oldest woman ski racer in the world!

16

Max's Mountain

The thought of leaving Colorado, of going back east or anywhere else, never entered our minds. There often were hard moments, but never enough to completely discourage us.

During our second decade at Ski Tip Ranch the entire town of Dillon was being torn down because of the building of the new dam. I remember a big sign over a gas station in Dillon:

WE'RE DOOMED TO BE DAMNED
BUT DAMMED IF WE'RE DOOMED

Since Dillon would be inundated that would eliminate the grade school, but not until our children finished eighth grade. Bestemor offered to take Rolf and Sunni during their high school years, so she bought a small house in Aspen on the main street for $9,500. It has since become Arthur's Chinese Restaurant.

Bestemor, now 80 years young, welcomed the idea of the children living with her and attending Aspen High. What a lucky choice this was. Both Rolf and Sunni were on the Aspen Junior ski team with classmates, Myke Baar, Billy Marolt (who became Alpine Director of the U.S. Ski Team), Jimmy Huega, and Sharon Pejak. Some would be with them through college years.

All the years while Sunni and Rolf were in school we had wondered about the enormous expense of sending them to college. Sunni, valedictorian of her class, and salutatorian, Ellen Feinsinger, became roommates at Pomona College where Sunni won a full scholarship. Rolf, who majored in fine arts and did the paintings in this book, received an athletic scholarship at the University of Denver where he was on the ski team.

Our close friends, Peter Seibert, and Fitzhugh and Eileen Scott, almost convinced us to move to Vail, the new, big ski area, but throughout the years Max persisted in his determination to make Keystone Mountain a ski area. Therefore we had approached the U.S. Forest Service on the possibility of developing the mountain. The current ranger, however, advised us to wait until after the Peak One mountain south of Frisco became a reality as a ski area. "Frisco needs this for economic reasons," we were told.

Our good friend, Dale Gallagher of the Forest Service, we felt, would give us the best advice. After listening to us and looking over Max's new relief model of Keystone Mountain, he made this comment, "Time is of the essence. If you want to develop Keystone you'd better move fast."

The uphill part began with trying to raise money to get Keystone going. Max's first small corporation was successful in getting the Forest Service study permit and tying up the land at the base. Beyond that, it all needed much more financial backing.

Fortunately our good ski friends from Iowa, Jane and Bill Bergman, stopped in one evening for cocktails. Hearing talk of the problems, they asked to see Max's model of the mountain.

After viewing the model, Bill said, "Max, I think I can put together a corporation to get the job done. I know a company which can do it if anyone can. I've already put together one small corporation for them which was successful. I don't think they'll be afraid to tackle this. If anyone can do it right, they can."

"What's the company?" Max asked.

"It's the Ralston Purina Company."

For years we had looked up at the wooded slopes of Keystone Mountain with the late afternoon sun making deep blue shadows in the gulleys and varying terrain of the mountain. Max realized that now, with the support of a large corporation, we would someday ski on *his* mountain. Being an eternal optimist, Max had never given up. However, I

208

Max walks every inch of his mountain, laying out the trails.

Keystone Ski School Director—1970-1975

209

Dercums named to Hall of Fame

British Royalty Entrains for Castle Yuletide

Together, we are honored by being inducted into the Colorado Ski Hall of Fame in 1980.

We come full cycle. Keystone buys Arapahoe over 30 years after Arapahoe began and Max christens the new triple lift.

210

confess I often had feared that it would never materialize.

As soon as the Keystone Corporation became a reality, Max started to walk the mountain. "The only way the trails can be laid out correctly, Edna," he told me one day, "is to know the entire mountain."

Every morning Max would put on elastic knee bandages to prevent any knee strain or injuries. He took no risks because he knew he would become Director of the Keystone Ski School. It was rough terrain over downed logs through thick timber. Fortunately there were a few logging roads where he could drive the jeep. To know the best terrain for ski trails he needed to crisscross the entire mountain.

One Sunday morning Max drove me part way up the mountain. "Now we'll walk to where I have found a surprise for you." After climbing over fallen logs through mossy ground and over small streams he finally came to a stop. "There," Max pointed. "Look at that perfect little bonsai spruce." Carefully he dug it up and put it safely in a gunnysack to take home.

As it all began to come together I gradually realized how important it was for the quality of his planning that Max was a forester, a skier, and during the war, a logger. Also his talents as an artist and draftsman made it possible for him to create the relief model and paint a picture of the future ski area as he envisioned it. Other people could then appreciate the fantastic possibilities of Keystone. One evening I overheard Max telling some ski friends about Keystone. "I've been specially lucky to have people like Bill Bergman, Mel Bahle, and Hal Dean of Ralston Purina share my dream. I'm sure they're going to make it all possible."

The minister of the Interfaith Chapel at Vail, Colorado, Don Simonton, wrote about Max and Keystone in his article, "The Other Side of Skiing" which appeared in *SKIING Magazine,* in 1978.

> *Skiing with Max Dercum is a ski lesson, a trip through history, a course in ecology, most of all an experience of the special fraternity of skiing. Keystone is Max's mountain. It reflects his personal interest and his philosophy, a fascinating blend of recreation and ecology.*

His runs were designed with scenic profiles, the interplay of vegetation and vista, with a touch of adventure that you get by following the mountain's natural contours. He designed runs the whole family could enjoy—steep pitch for hotshot Junior, sweeping traverse around it for Mom.

Cruising the slopes with him involves constant observations about improvements of wildlife habitat by opening up the forest, watershed benefits from snowmaking and erosion control and sheltered clearings.

Max is typical of a whole generation of skiers. They obviously love skiing much more for its sun, snow, schuss, and sociability than for its fashions and foibles.

Today, while sitting on the terrace of the mall at Keystone Lodge enjoying a gourmet lunch, I look across the lake remembering it as a small beaver pond with the distant mountains reflected in the still water. Now I see reflected a number of attractive new condominiums. It is hard for me to think back and believe all this change.

Now we have both passed 65 and have retired from active ski-instructing and running Ski Tip Lodge. We are free to enjoy together skiing, racing, hiking, playing tennis, reading and traveling. Max treasures spending his time playing his clarinet, sketching, and painting. We are so busy enjoying our life that we wonder how we ever found time in the past to work.

Snug in our new home built high on the slope of Lenawee Mountain, we are a part of the dramatic view just up the road from Ski Tip Ranch.

It is late afternoon and I can hear Max's chain saw as he is busy clearing our own short practice slope behind the house. This will keep us both in shape for future ski seasons.

I wonder if we will get to ski in heaven? If Saint Peter gives me wings, I think I'll trade mine in for skis!

Some day Max will say to me, "Remember back 50 years ago, Edna, to your first race?" And I'll answer, "You know Max, it sure hasn't been easy all the time, but it has been downhill all the way."

212

Edna Strand Dercum *author*

born in Minnesota, attended the University of Minnesota and Penn State College, where she met her husband, Max. They live just up the road from Ski Tip Ranch at 10,000 feet elevation in their home which they refer to as "a roof folded over a dramatic view," built by their son-in-law, Alf Tieze.

At Age 67 she tells:

> *One of the joys of having the 4 generations living close by, is*
> *seeing our 5 grandchildren involved in skiing and climbing*
> *the same mountains our children did. It is a beautiful*
> *reminder of our early years here. Plus, getting together at Ski*
> *Tip, which son Rolf now runs. Or maybe it runs him, as it*
> *did me all those years.*

Max Dercum *illustrator*

was born in Ohio and graduated from Cornell University in 1934. In 1942, after 7 years as Professor of Forestry at Penn State, he decided to move his family out west, where he became involved in mining, logging, ranching and the ski world of Colorado. Retired today at age 69, he enjoys, aside from skiing, his clarinet, playing tennis, sketching and his model railroad hobby.

Rolf Dercum *painter*

Max and Edna's son, describes the inspiration and motivation in his art:

> *It all started in this mountain valley—from my grandfather*
> *the desire to become an artist, from my father an awareness*
> *and love of nature. I wish to leave an appreciation of the*
> *changing moods of nature to my children through my paintings*
> *of our own mountains, woods, and beaver meadows.*

Edna says, *No way would this book have been completed without. . .*

Jean Valens Bullard *editor*

who envisioned what the book could be, and helped bring out the best in the story as well as playing a part in it over the years,

Christina Watkins *designer*

who enhances the book with artistic skills and sensitivity,

. . . and gratitude to those who wrote articles and news items about Ski Tip, Arapahoe and Keystone, especially, I. Wm. Berry, *Skier's Almanac,* Abby Rand, Mort Lund and Charlie Meyers in *Ski Magazine,* plus Rev. Don Simonton and John Jerome in *Skiing Magazine,* and Joanne Ditmer in the *Denver Post,* to Larry Monninger for the color picture of Ski Tip, and to Cliff Gibbs, last but not least, for many of the photos and for creating havoc in the kitchen with his Mt. St. Helens pancakes.

213